TRUTH *radicality*

AND BEYOND IN CONTEMPORARY ARCHITECTURE

Jeff Koons,
Living Sculpture:
Dog in front of the Guggenheim Bilbao
consisting of live plants and flowers.
A small gate at the bottom allows
access to the gardener who tends the
flowers and watering system.
Photograph, AP-NA

Philip Johnson & Alan Ritchie, Turning Point,
Case Western Reserve University,
Cleveland, Ohio

NEW**ARCHITECTURE 5**

TRUTH *radicality*

AND BEYOND IN CONTEMPORARY ARCHITECTURE

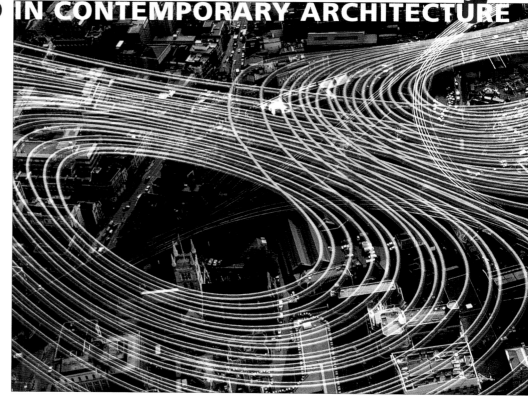

Nigel Coates & Doug Branson,
Ecstacity

ANDREAS PAPADAKIS PUBLISHER

NEW**ARCHITECTURE**
Number 5   July 2000

Head Office, 107 Park Street
London W1Y 3FB, United Kingdom

Tel.   +44 (0)20 7499 0444
Fax   +44 (0)20 7499 0222
email: papadakis@btinternet.com

Editor-in-Chief
Andreas Papadakis

House Editor: Vicky Braouzou
Assistant: Alex Papadakis
Administration: Sarah Williams

NEW**ARCHITECTURE** is available by subscription and in bookshops worldwide.
Subscription rates for six numbers (including p&p) are £90.00/US$135. Individual
issues are available at £17.50/US$27.50

Printed and bound in Singapore

TOP LEFT: Panel at the BA Bienal. From left to right: Franco Purini, Cesar Pelli, Ricardo Legorreta, Jorge Glusberg, P. Josef Kleihues, Andreas Papadakis TOP RIGHT: Cesar Pelli ABOVE LEFT: Ricardo Legorreta ABOVE MIDDLE: Massimiliano Fuksas ABOVE RIGHT: Alan Ritchie and Philip Johnson at their office, New York

contents

ACKNOWLEDGMENTS

We are grateful to Jean Baudrillard for permission to translate and publish his lecture *Vérité ou Radicalité de l'architecture*, and to Sage Publications for permission to reproduce an image and extract from *Art and Artefact* edited by N. Zurbrugg.
Several articles were either presented at the BA Bienal or commissioned on the basis of events there. With its 70 contributing architects and critics it is difficult to do justice to the event.

We would like to thank those members of our editorial board who have contributed articles or work, including Kenneth Frampton, Hans Hollein, Daniel Libeskind, and Hani Rashid. We are most grateful to Philip Johnson for his warm welcome and for giving us to much of this time on several occasions in New York and Canaan, and to his partner Alan Ritchie; to Christie's for photographs of the Rockefeller Guesthouse; and to Dimitri Fatouros for a memorable brainstorming session.

The essay by Lionel March is based on his keynote lecture at the Greenwich 2000 International Symposium on Digital Creativity.
The Pompidou Centre and Renzo Piano kindly provided material and illustrations from their exhibition; and the excellent press office at Tate Modern facilities and material for publication. Many photos of the Tate were taken specially by Grant Smith and NA staff. We are grateful to Christo and Jeanne-Claude for their hospitality in New York and to Ms Annely Juda who

organized their exhibition *Black and White* at her London gallery.
We wish to thank the offices of those architects featured who were kind enough to provide illustrations and material for publication; and Christian Richters and Hélène Binet for the photographs of Zaha Hadid's work. Our warm thanks to Jazmin Agostini for her hard work in assembling the initial material from the BA Bienal.

Cover: *Toyo Ito, JVC contemporary art, design and architecture centre, Mexico.*

TOP LEFT: Wolf Prix at the BA Bienal TOP MIDDLE: Leon Krier. TOP RIGHT: Zaha Hadid and Jorge Glusberg. ABOVE LEFT: Alvaro Siza, at the RIBA. ABOVE MIDDLE: Jacques Herzog and Harry Gugger at the inauguration of Tate Modern. ABOVE RIGHT: Daniel Libeskind at the inauguration of the Jewish Museum, Berlin

Possible and Impossible

Andreas Papadakis

"There is a future for architecture for the simple reason that we have not yet invented the building, the architectural object that will put an end to all the rest, that will put an end to space itself; nor have we invented the city that will put an end to all cities, nor the thought that will put an end to all thought."
Jean Baudrillard

Jean Baudrillard reassuringly set the tone with his keynote lecture at the BA Bienal "*Vérité ou Radicalité de l'Architecture*." There still exists, he insists, beyond all illusion and disillusion, a future for architecture even if that future is not necessarily architectural as we know it.

In preparing this issue we selected in part from the contributions of the some 70 international architects and critics who were invited to contribute their own vision of contemporary architecture at the Bienal by the ever dynamic Jorge Glusberg, director of the Buenos Aires Fine Arts Museum.

The majority of speakers, far from lamenting the demise of architecture, reveal their strong determination to press forward and develop new ideas for the future.

Take, for example, Wolf Prix: using language reminiscent of Marinetti's 1909 Manifesto he follows his own revolutionary line and urges "Think the impossible."

The pursuit of the impossible and the innovative is a common current in architectural theory and practice today at a time when constraints have vanished and technology no longer dazzles with its dominance. Nevertheless, the presence of technology still colours the landscape as is evident from Renzo Piano's recent exhibition at the Pompidou Centre and, most prominently in Britain, with the work of Norman Foster. Other examples of today's tendencies are Zaha Hadid's fluid forms, Hasegawa's intimate dialogue with the landscape, and Toyo Ito's minimalist gestures.

But perhaps the most provocative and significant ideas today come from a young man of 94. Since his aptly named "Turning Point" (Case Western University), Philip Johnson has been creating a sense of wonder with unfamiliar shapes, some reminiscent of medieval buttressing. In his Cathedral of Hope the designs are more complex, the sombre exterior in contrast with the sensuous design of the interior with its niches and "protected" spaces. A sophisticated solution for special needs.

Nevertheless, to complete the story, however provocative an architect may be in his own work, he frequently has to accept that the past is ever present and solutions have to be found that can accommodate something close to symbiosis. We offer two examples: London's newly opened Tate Modern where Herzog and de Meuron have developed a solution that lives happily with Sir Giles Gilbert Scott's former power station; and Daniel Libeskind's Jewish Museum in San Francisco where he has had to content himself with a traditional warehouse which he has transformed to accommodate his own concepts.

David Nash R.A.
***Pyramid, Sphere, Cube,** 1999*
A large oak sculpture with accompanying charcoal drawings purchased by the Chantrey Bequest for the Tate. It forms the centrepiece of Gallery VI at the Summer Exhibition at the Royal Academy of Arts in London, reputed to be the largest open contemporary art exhibition in the world where over 100,000 visitors are expected. This annual event reflects the mood of professional and gifted amateur artists. Many works are for sale and sales should exceed £2 million.
Among distinguished international artists exhibiting, Eduardo Paolozzi and Frank Stella have dedicated spaces for their work. Architects include Norman Foster, Richard Rogers and Peter Cook.

"... for me photography has nothing to do with finding a particular vision or a subjective style in order to interpret the world. Rather, it is a process of capturing things, because objects are themselves captivating. It's almost like trapping things – like trying to catch the primitive dimension of an object, as opposed to the secondary dimension of the subject and the whole domain of representation. It's the immanent presence of the object, rather than the representation of the subject."

Jean Baudrillard, from an interview with Nicholas Zurbrugg

St Clément, 1998

From the 'Ecstasy of Photography', a series of exhibitions of Baudrillard's photographs, in Brisbane, Sydney, Adelaide and Melbourne, featured in 'Art and Artefact', edited by Nicholas Zurbrugg (Sage Publications).

See also under 'Books' in Cosmorama.

Jean Baudrillard

Vérité ou Radicalité de l' Architecture
Truth or Radicality in Architecture

Let us begin with space, which is after all the primal arena of architecture, and with the radicality of space, which is the void. Is it necessary, is it possible to structure, to organise this space other than by extending it indefinitely either horizontally or vertically? In other words, when confronted with the radicality of space, is it possible to invent truth in architecture?

Does architecture peter out in its reality, in its references, in its procedures, in its functions, in its techniques? Or does it go beyond all that and lose itself in something else, which is perhaps its own end, or something that might permit it to go beyond its own end? Does architecture exist beyond truth, beyond its own truth, in a sort of radicality that challenges space – rather than controls it – that challenges society in its obedience of its conventions and institutions, that challenges the very creation of architecture and the creative architect with his illusion of control.

I wanted to define architectural illusion in its two contradictory meanings: when it creates an illusion and is indeed itself an illusion; and when it invents a fresh illusion, a new illusion of the city and space, another arena where it exceeds its brief.

Personally, I am above all interested in space and in everything that in so-called built objects gives me a vertiginous sense of space. And so it is buildings such as the Pompidou Centre, the World Trade Center and Biosphere II that interest me, not because they are architectural masterpieces – it wasn't

their architectural significance that captivated me – but the fact that, like the majority of our great contemporary architectural objects, they seem to have been parachuted from another world. What truth do they have? If, for example, I take the truth of a building like the two towers of the World Trade Center, I see that the architecture of that time, the 1960s, draws the profile of a hyperreal but not yet computerised society and period. The two towers already resemble two perforated cards in their twinness. Today we could say that they were already the sign, the clone of each other. Are they a precursor of our age? And in that case is the architect working not with reality but with fiction, in an anticipatory illusion of our society? Or is he simply translating what is already there? It is in this sense that I asked the question: Is there truth in architecture in the sense of a suprasensible intended purpose of architecture and space?

Let us try and see what there is in this creative illusion, in what is beyond reality in architecture. The architect's adventure takes place in a real world. He is in a particular situation that is not that of the traditional artist. He is not someone who pores over blank pages or a blank canvas. He has to create in a limited time, to a fixed budget, for specific people an object that is not always defined in advance. He works with a team in a situation where he has direct or indirect safety, financial and professional constraints.

Partons de l'espace, qui est quand même la scène primitive de l'architecture, et de la radicalité de l'espace, qui est le vide. Y-a-t-il nécessité, y-a-t-il possibilité, de structurer, d'organiser cet espace autrement que par une extension horizontale et verticale indéfinie? Autrement dit, est-il possible d'inventer, face à la radicalité de l'espace, une vérité de l'architecture?

Est-ce que l'architecture s'épuise dans sa réalité, dans ses références, dans ses procédures, dans ses fonctions, dans ses techniques? Ou est-ce qu'elle n'excède pas tout cela pour s'épuiser dans autre chose qui serait sa propre fin ou qui lui permettrait d'aller au-delà de sa fin? Est-ce que l'architecture existe encore au-delà de sa propre vérité, au-delà de

sa réalité propre, dans une sorte de radicalité de défi à l'espace – et non pas seulement de gestion de l'espace – de défi à cette société non pas seulement d'obéissance à ses conventions et à ses institutions, de défi à la création architecturale elle-même, à l'architecte créateur, et à l'illusion de maîtrise.

Voilà, je voulais cerner ce qu'il en est de l'illusion architecturale dans un double sens complètement opposé là où elle fait illusion et se fait illusion sur elle-même et là où elle invente une illusion nouvelle, l'illusion neuve de la cité et de l'espace, une autre scène qui la dépasse elle-même.

Personnellement moi je suis surtout intéressé à l'espace et à tout ce qui dans les objets dit construits me rend le vertige de l'espace. Ce sont

donc plutôt des objets tels que Beaubourg, le World Trade Center, la Biosphère II, etc. qui m'ont intéressé, c'est-à-dire des objets qui n'etaient pas exactement des merveilles architecturales pour moi, ce n'etait pas leur sens architectural qui me captivait, mais ces objets semblaient comme parachutés d'un autre monde. C'est d'ailleurs le cas de la plupart de nos grands objets architecturaux contemporains. Et quelle est leur vérité? Si je prends par exemple la vérité d'un édifice comme les deux tours du World Trade Center je vois qu'à ce moment-là, dès les anneés 60 l'architecture dessine le profil d'une société et d'une époque hyperréelle sinon informatisée et ces deux tours ont l'air déjà de deux cartes perforées

dans leurs jumellité. On pourrait dire aujourd'hui qu'elles étaient déjà le signe, le clone, l'une de l'autre. Sont-elles une anticipation de notre temps? Est-ce que l'architecte est donc non pas dans la réalité mais dans la fiction, une société dans l'illusion anticipatrice? Ou bien, est-ce qu'il traduit tout simplement ce qui est déjà là. C'est dans ce sens que je posais la question: Est-ce qu'il y a une vérité de l'architecture au sens d'une destination supra sensible de l'architecture et de l'espace?

Essayons de voir ce qu'il en est de cette illusion créatrice, de cet au-delà de la réalité architecturale. L'aventure de l'architecte se situe dans un monde qui est bien réel. Il est dans une situation bien particulière qui n'est pas celui d'un

Under these circumstances, what scope is there for freedom, for circumventing the constraints? The problem is to articulate each project according to a prior concept or idea using a very specific strategy to define a place that one does not know. We are in the field of invention, of non-knowledge, of risk and, in the end, this place can become a place of secrecy, of things not under control, which belong in the realm of fate or the voluntary surrender of control. This is where overt illusion comes into play: the illusion of a space which is not only visible but which may be the mental prolongation of what we see. The basic hypothesis here is that architecture is not what fills a space but what generates space, whether by misappropriation, by isolation, or by an almost unconscious conjuring trick. But from then on the mind plays its part. Take a Japanese garden, where there is always a vanishing point, a place where one does not know if the garden ends or continues. Or again, take Jean Nouvel's Tower without End for La Défense in Paris. It is an attempt to go beyond the logic of the Albertian perspective, in other words to organise all the elements in such a way that they can be read in a scale progression and make one conscious of space. The fact that the Tower disappears into the sky, goes beyond the boundary of the immaterial, and is at the limits of the tangible and of perception is part of an architecture that is not virtual (although the Tower has remained virtual in that it has never been built). But it has created more than one can see. It is a seductive mental space for the eye and for the mind. In the Fondation Cartier, also by Jean Nouvel, the facade is larger than the building and I do not know if I am looking at the sky itself or at the sky through transparent glass. If I look at a tree through three layers of glass, I do not know whether I am looking at a tree through glass or at the reflection of a tree. And when two trees are lined up in relation to the glass, I do not know if there is a second tree and if it is a real tree.

This form of illusion is not gratuitous. Through the destabilisation of perception it permits the creation of a mental space, and the installation of a setting, a scenic space, without which, as we know, buildings would be merely constructions and the city itself an agglomeration of constructions. All our cities suffer from this loss of scene and thus of the whole dramaturgy of illusion and seduction because their space is filled with functional architecture, some useful some useless.

A presentation of the Issey Miyake collection at the Fondation Cartier provided a good illustration of the object in a stage setting, for the transparency of this architectural object gives it the role of an actor. Scene One – Issey Miyake's creations moving through the interior space. Then the gallery full of guests – the majority of them women in Issey Miyake – are also, without knowing it, part of the same scene. Then the building itself, which reflects all this and, finally, everything together seen from the outside forming one spectacle, with the exhibition space becoming an exhibit and thus invisible.

It seems to me that this quality of being present but at the same time invisible is a fundamental quality, for it is this form of what could be called secret invisibility that most effectively counteracts hegemonic visibility, that dictatorship of the transparent in which everything must be visible and legible and where the problem is to invest mental and visual space, which is no longer a space for seeing but a space to be seen.

This assumes an architecture capable of creating both place and non place and of maintaining the prestige of the transparent without exercising its dictatorship, which results in unidentified, unidentifiable objects that challenge the surrounding order and have a dual, conflicting relationship with the real order. It is in this sense that we can speak not of their truth but of their radicality. If this duel does not take place, if architecture has to be the functional, programmatic transcription of the constraints posed by the social and urban order then it no longer exists as architecture. A successful object is one that has an existence beyond its own reality and that creates for the public user a dual relationship (not merely an interactive one) consisting of misappropriation, contradiction and destabilisation.

if architecture has to be the functional, programmatic transcription of the constraints posed by the social and urban order then it no longer exists as architecture.

artiste au sens traditionnel. Ce n'est pas quelqu'un qui médite devant sa feuille blanche ou qui travaille devant sa toile. Il doit produire dans un temps précis, avec un budget donné, pour des personnes données un objet qui lui peut-être n'est pas donné à l'avance. Il travaille avec une équipe. Il est donc dans une situation où il va être censuré de façon directe ou indirecte, au nom de la sécurité, au nom de l'argent, au nom du corps professionnel.

A partir de là, où est l'espace de liberté, où est le moyen de dépasser ces contraintes? Le problème est d'articuler chaque projet à un concept ou à une idée préalable avec une stratégie très particulière qui va définir un lieu qu'on ne connaît pas. On est dans le domaine de l'invention, dans le domaine du non savoir, dans le domaine du risque; et ce lieu finalement peut devenir le lieu d'un certain secret, de choses qu'on ne maîtrise pas, de l'ordre du fatal ou du volontairement incontrôlé. Là commence l'illusion ouverte, celle d'un espace qui n'est pas seulement visible mais qui serait le prolongement mental de ce qu'on voit. L'hypothèse de base étant que l'architecture n'est pas ce qui remplit un espace mais ce qui génère de l'espace. Cela peut être par des détournements,

par la mise en abîme, par une prestidigitation presque inconsciente, mais à partir de là l'esprit fonctionne. Voyez les jardins japonais où il y a toujours un point de fuite, un endroit où on ne sait pas si le jardin s'arrête ou s'il continue. Ou encore dans la tentative de Jean Nouvel dans la Tour sans fin de la Défense, cette tentative de dépasser la logique de la perspective albertienne, autrement dit d'organiser tous les éléments de façon qu'ils se lisent dans une progression d'échelle et fassent prendre conscience de l'espace. Que la Tour se perde dans le ciel, ce passage à la limite de l'immatériel, aux confins du sensible et de la perception, fait partie d'une architecture qui n'est pas du tout du virtuel, encore que la Tour est restée virtuelle, puisqu'elle n'a jamais été construite bien entendu, mais qui s'est créée plus que ce que l'on voit. Pour l'oeil et pour l'esprit c'est un espace mental de séduction. Dans la Fondation Cartier du même Jean Nouvel, si je regarde la façade, comme la façade est plus grande que le bâtiment, je ne sais pas si je vois le ciel ou le ciel en transparence. Si je regarde un arbre à travers trois plans vitrés, je ne sais jamais si je vois l'arbre en transparence ou le reflet de

l'arbre. Et quand deux arbres entrent comme par hasard en parallèle par rapport à un plan vitré, je ne sais jamais s'il y a un deuxième arbre ou si c'est un arbre réel.

Cette forme d'illusion n'est pas gratuite. Elle permet par la déstabilisation de la perception de créer un espace mental, d'y instaurer une scène, un espace scénique, sans lequel, comme on sait, les édifices ne seraient que des constructions et la ville elle-même une agglomération. Et c'est bien de cette perte de la scène, et donc du regard, et donc de toute une dramaturgie de l'illusion et de la séduction dont souffrent toutes nos villes vouées à la saturation de l'espace par une architecture de fonction, utile ou inutile d'ailleurs.

La dernière présentation des modèles Issey Miyake à la Fondation Cartier était une belle illustration de cette mise en scène de l'objet où l'objet architectural loin de s'imposer et d'imposer son espace joue comme acteur grâce à sa transparence vivante. Première scène, les créations Issey Miyake mobiles dans l'espace intérieur. Puis la galerie des invités, les femmes – dont la plupart en Issey Miyake d'ailleurs – figurant sans le savoir dans la même mise en scène. Puis l'édifice lui-même qui

reflète tout cela, et enfin tout cela ensemble vu de l'extérieur comme une action globale, l'espace d'exposition devenant lui-même un objet exposé et finissant ainsi par se rendre invisible.

Je pense que c'est cette capacité d'être là et en même temps de se faire invisible qui est une qualité fondamentale car c'est cette forme on pourrait dire d'invisibilité secrète qui met en échec le plus efficacement la visibilité hégémonique, cette dictature de la transparence où tout doit se faire visible et déchiffrable où tout le problème est d'investir l'espace mental et visuel, lequel n'est plus alors celui du voir mais du faire voir.

A quoi suppose une architecture capable de créer à la fois le lieu et le non lieu et de garder les prestiges de la transparence sans en exercer la dictature. Il en résulte des objets non identifiés, non identifiables qui sont un défi à l'ordre environnant, qui sont en relations duelles, éventuellement conflictuelles, avec l'ordre réel. C'est en ce sens qu'on peut parler non de leur vérité mais de leur radicalité. Si ce duel n'a pas lieu, si l'architecture doit être à la transcription fonctionnelle et programmatique des contraintes de l'ordre social et urbain, alors elle n'existe plus

The problem is the same in the fields of philosophy and writing, and in the political and social order. In all of them and whatever one does one cannot choose an event; one can choose only the concept. But that remains. The concept inevitably enters into conflict with the context, with all the positive, functional meanings that a building or a theory or indeed anything else can assume. The concept is something that in relation to the event as it presents itself, as it is interpreted or over-interpreted by the media and the news, creates a non-event. It sets a theoretical and fictional non-event against a so-called real event.

Naturally I understand better how this happens with regard to writing. I see it less well for architecture but in the case of certain objects I feel this kind of illusion, of extrapolation, of another space, another setting, as an aspiration required by each project and each functional constraint. I think it is the only solution to the impossible exchange of space and city, a solution that is obviously not to be found in the artificial spaces that have been created there.

This brings us to the question of the destiny of architecture when it lays claim to certain truths. What happens to the search for truth, that is to the determined ambition to fulfil a programme, to meet social and political needs, to transform social data with a cultural, pedagogic mission, etc.; in short, to all those things that feed official discourse and that relate to the conscious will of the architect himself? Fortunately or unfortunately, what we see is that the goals of the programmes are always misappropriated by those for whom they were intended, that is by the user, by that mass of people whose original or perverse response can never be written into the project. There is no automatic writing of social relations or mass needs, either in politics or architecture. Here too there is always a duel and the reaction is unpredictable. It is the reaction of a major player whom there is often a tendency to include as a passive element but who does not necessarily obey the rules of the game or the laws of dialogue. The masses take over the architectural object in their own way and even if the architect himself has not been diverted from his programme, the object will be diverted in any case, for its users will ensure that they restore to it the unpredictable destiny that it lacked. This, too, is a form of radicality albeit an involuntary one.

In this way all the intentions behind the Pompidou Centre have been thwarted by the object itself. A project that was based on positive perspectives – culture, communication – in the end succumbed to the reality – the hyper reality – of the object itself. Massive usage contradicted all the human and cultural aims of the project. Instead of being contextual it has created a void around it. Its flexible, scattered spaces, its transparency that was supposed to be in tune with modern man, came face to face with the masses who rendered it opaque and abused it in their own way. Contradiction has thus played the wild card and for the Pompidou has provided a sort of destiny.

The object, the true object, carries within it a certain fatality from which doubtless one should not attempt to escape. This calls into question the control of the creator, as it should. Just when he is tempted to add his signature to a function and a place, that is to fill a space according to a fixed plan, the other, all the others, will ensure that they make it a non-place and empty it of all meaning, by inventing new rules. This is in a way immoral but, as we know, it is neither morality nor a positive value system that enables a society to advance, but rather immorality and vice. There must exist in the imaginary as well as in space an ineluctable curve that runs counter to any planning, reality, or programming. In such circumstances the architect himself can play at thwarting his own plans but he cannot claim to control the object as an event, the symbolic rule being that the player must never be greater than the game itself. We are all players. That is to say that what we hope for most intensely is that from time to time rational links will unravel and for just a brief moment be replaced by an unexpected sequence of a different order, a wonderful outstripping of events, an extraordinary, pre-destined succession where one has the impression that things

en tant que telle. Un objet réussi c'est celui qui existe au-delà de sa propre réalité qui crée, y compris envers le public usager, une relation duelle, non seulement interactive faite de détournements, de contradictions, de déstabilisations.

Le problème est le même dans l'ordre de la pensée et de l'écriture, dans l'ordre politique et social. Partout et quoiqu'on fasse on n'a pas le choix de l'événement. On n'a que le choix du concept. Mais celui-là on le garde. Le concept c'est quelque chose qui doit forcément entrer en conflit avec le contexte, avec toutes les significations positives, fonctionnelles que peut prendre un édifice ou une théorie ou n'importe quoi d'autre. Le concept c'est quelque chose qui par rapport à l'événement tel qu'il se donne, tel qu'il est déchiffré et surdéchiffré par les média et par l'information, crée le non événement. Il oppose à l'événement soi-disant réel un non événement théorique et fictionnel.

Pour l'écriture évidemment je vois mieux comment cela peut se passer. Je le vois moins bien pour l'architecture mais dans certains objets je ressens cette sorte d'illusion, d'extrapolation d'un autre espace, d'une autre scène, une aspiration que demandent tout projet et toute contrainte fonctionnelle. Seule solution je pense à l'échange impossible de l'espace et de la ville qu'on ne trouvera évidemment pas dans les espaces artificiels de liberté qu'on y a aménagés.

Ici se pose la question même du destin de l'architecture lorsqu'elle prétend à quelques vérités. Qu'advient-il du projet de vérité, c'est-à-dire de l'ambition déterminée de remplir un programme, de répondre à des besoins sociaux et politiques, d'être un transformateur des données sociales avec mission culturelle, pédagogique, etc. Bref, tout ce qui nourrit le discours officiel et qui touche à la volonté consciente de l'architecte lui-même. Et bien, heureusement ou malheureusement, on s'aperçoit que ces finalités programmées sont toujours détournées par ceux mêmes à qui elles sont destinées, par l'usager, par cette masse dont la réponse originale ou perverse ne peut jamais être inscrite dans le projet. Il n'y a pas d'écriture automatique de la relation sociale, des besoins de masse ni en politique ni en architecture. Là aussi il y a toujours un duel et la réaction est imprévisible. C'est la réaction d'un acteur à part entière qu'on a souvent tendance à inclure comme élément passif mais qui n'obéit pas forcément à la règle du jeu ou aux lois du dialogue. Les masses s'emparent de l'objet architectural à leur façon et si l'architecte ne s'est pas détourné lui-même de son programme, l'objet sera détourné de toute façon et les usagers se chargeront de lui rendre cette destination imprévisible qui lui fait défaut. Là aussi il y a une forme de radicalité mais involontaire.

C'est ainsi que toutes les intentions qui ont fondé le projet Beaubourg ont été démenties par l'objet. Basé sur les perspectives positives – la culture, la communication – le projet a été finalement complètement traversé par la réalité, par l'hyperréalité de l'objet lui-même. L'usage massif aura contredit toutes les intentions humanistes et culturelles du projet. Au lieu d'être contextuel il a fait le vide autour de lui. Avec ses espaces flexibles, dispersés, sa transparence censée être en face avec les peuples modernes, il se retire une masse qui est venue l'opacifier et en abuser à sa façon. La contradiction aura donc joué d'une façon sauvage et cela aura été pour Beaubourg une sorte de destin.

L'objet, le véritable objet, est porteur d'une certaine fatalité à laquelle il ne faut sans doute pas vouloir échapper. Ceci remet en cause la maîtrise du créateur et c'est bien ainsi. Là où il est tenté de signer une fonction et un lieu, donc de remplir un espace selon un plan déterminé, les autres, tous les autres, se chargeront d'en refaire un non lieu, de le vider de sa signification, d'inventer une autre règle du jeu. Ceci est en quelque sorte immoral mais, comme on sait, ce n'est ni la moralité ni le système positif des valeurs d'une société qui la fait progresser. C'est son immoralité et ses vices. Il doit y avoir dans l'imaginaire aussi, comme dans l'espace, une courbure inéluctable qui s'oppose à toute planification, à toute linéarité, à toute programmation. Dans cette conjoncture, l'architecte lui-même peut jouer à déjouer ses propres plans mais il ne peut prétendre maîtriser l'objet comme événement, la règle symbolique étant que jamais le joueur ne doit être plus grand que le jeu lui-même. Nous sommes tous joueurs. C'est-à-dire que nous espérons ce que nous espérons le plus intensément, c'est que se défassent de temps en temps les enchaînements rationnels et que s'installent même pour un temps bref un déroulement inouï, d'un autre ordre, une surenchère merveilleuse, des événements, une succession extraordinaire comme prédestinée ou

until then maintained artificially apart, are suddenly no longer random but converge and run together spontaneously at the same intensity because they are interconnected. Our world would be unliveable without this power of divergence, without this radicality from elsewhere, from the object not the subject, and without this strange attraction.

I think that architects themselves find it seductive to imagine that the buildings that they build, the spaces they invent, are places that are secret, random, unpredictable, poetic in a way, and not just official places resulting from the sociologists' statistics. That said, we are now confronted in our contemporary world – and this is valid in all fields not only architecture – by a quite different dimension, a dimension where the question of truth and of radicality is not even posed because we have crossed over into the realm of virtuality. And here there is a major risk, which is that archi-

> **architecture has become a simple operator of visibility, screen architecture, and to some extent instead of being the natural intelligence of space and city it has become their artificial intelligence.**

tecture no longer exists at all, that there is no more of it. There are different ways for architecture not to exist. Man conceived and built his environment according to spontaneous rules and this inhabited space was not made for contemplation. It had no aesthetic value. Even today what pleases me in certain American cities is that architecture has been forgotten. One can travel through them without ever thinking about architecture. One can move around in them as in a desert without the make-believe of art, of the history of art, of aesthetics, of architecture. These cities permit a return to a primitive form of space. They are, of course, structured for multiple purposes but, as they are, they are like a pure event, a pure object, and not that pretence of archi-tecture that sets itself on a pedestal. In this sense it is architecture that plays the role of anti architecture. What is more, Rem Koolhaas's famous book *Delirious New York* reveals how Manhattan was built on the basis of something that had nothing architectural about it, the Coney Island amusement park. For me that is perfect architecture which by its dimensions removes any trace of itself and where space

represents thought itself. This is valid for art also, and for painting. There is no stronger work than one that has no pretensions to be art, history of art, aesthetics. And it is the same thing for thought. There is no thought stronger than that which no longer has pretensions of profundity or the history of ideas or truth.

But with the virtual we are no longer dealing with architecture that knows how to play on the visible and the invisible and to keep a secret, with architecture as symbolic form playing simultaneously with mass and gravity and their disappearance. It is architecture that no longer has any secrets at all, that has become a simple operator of visibility, screen architecture, and to some extent instead of being the natural intelligence of space and city it has become their artificial intelligence. I have nothing against artificial intelligence except when it claims in its universal calculation to absorb all other forms and to reduce mental space to numeric space. To evaluate this risk, which is also the risk that the adventure of architecture will end, I shall take an example from another field with which I am more familiar, that of photography. According to Wilhelm Flusser's hypothesis the great majority of photographic images today represent neither a choice nor a vision of the subject of the image but a simple extension of the technical virtuality of the camera. It is the machine that is in control, that seeks out all the possibilities. Man is merely the technician of the programme. That is the meaning of virtual. It uses up all the technical virtualities of the camera. This analysis can be extended to the computer and to artificial intelligence where in most cases thought is merely a combination of logistics, the virtual and infinite working of the machine. And so everything that results from technique and the immense possibilities for diversification it provides leads to an automatic representation of the world. And this is also true of architecture when it is exposed to all the technical possi-bilities. And I do not mean only materials and construction techniques but also form. Just as all images are possible with a camera – which makes no demands except to function – so all

on a l'impression que les choses jusque-là maintenues artificiellement à distance, d'un coup se retrouvent non pas livrées au hasard mais spontanément convergentes et concourant à la même intensité par leur enchaînement même. Notre monde serait invivable sans cette puissance de détournement infuse, sans cette radicalité venue d'ailleurs, venue de l'objet et non plus du sujet, sans cette attraction étrange.

Il y a là je pense quelque chose de séduisant pour les architectes eux-mêmes d'imaginer que les édifices qu'ils construisent, les espaces qu'ils inventent sont le lieu de comportement secret, aléatoire, imprévisible, poétique en quelque sorte, et non pas seulement de comportement officiel que la sociologie comptabilise en termes de statistiques. Ceci dit, nous sommes affrontés dans notre monde contemporain, et ceci vaut pour tous les domaines non seulement pour l'architecture, à une toute autre dimension, une dimension où la question de la vérité et de la radicalité ne se pose même plus parce que nous sommes passés dans la virtualité. Et il y a un risque majeur, c'est que l'architecture n'existe plus du tout; c'est qu'il n'y en ait plus du tout. Il y a différentes façons pour

l'architecture de ne pas exister. Il y a toute une architecture qui se fait, qui s'est faite depuis des millénaires sans même une idée de l'architecture. Les hommes ont conçu et construit leur environnement selon des règles spontanées et cet espace vécu n'était pas fait pour être contemplé. Il n'avait même pas de valeur esthétique. Aujourd'hui encore ce qui me plaît moi dans certaines villes américaines c'est que l'architecture s'y fait oubliée. C'est qu'on peut les traverser sans penser à l'architecture. On peut circuler là-dedans comme dans un désert sans se donner la comédie de l'art, de l'histoire de l'art, de l'esthétique, de l'architecture. Ces villes, qui nous permettent de revenir à une scène primitive de l'espace, bien sûr elles sont structurées à des fins multiples mais telles qu'elles sont là elles sont comme un événement pur, un objet pur; elles n'ont pas cette prétention de l'architecture qui se donne autel. Dans ce sens c'est une architecture qui fait office d'anti architecture. On le voit d'ailleurs à partir du livre bien connu de Rem Koolhaas Delirious New York, comment Manhattan s'est édifié à partir de quelque chose qui n'avait rien d'architectural, le parc d'attractions de Coney Island. Pour moi c'est

là la perfection de l'architecture que celle qui par ses dimensions efface ses propres traces et où l'espace est la pensée même. Ceci est valable pour l'art aussi, pour la peinture. Il n'y a pas d'oeuvre plus forte que celle qui ne se donne plus la comédie de l'art, de l'histoire de l'art, de l'esthétique. Et c'est la même chose pour la pensée. Il n'y a pas de pensée forte que celle qui ne se donne plus la comédie du sens et de la profondeur, ou la comédie de l'histoire des idées, ou la comédie de la vérité.

Mais avec le virtuel il ne s'agit plus du tout d'une architecture qui sait jouer sur le visible et l'invisible et garder son secret, une architecture comme forme symbolique qui joue à la fois avec la pesanteur, la gravité des choses et avec leur disparition. Il s'agit d'une architecture qui n'a plus de secret du tout, qui est devenue une simple opératrice de visibilité, une architecture écran et en quelque sorte au lieu d'en être l'intelligence naturelle devenue l'intelligence artificielle de l'espace et de la ville. Je n'ai rien contre l'intelligence artificielle sauf lorsqu'elle prétend dans son calcul universel absorber toutes les autres formes et réduire l'espace mental à un espace numérique.

Pour évaluer ce risque, qui est en même temps le risque de la fin de l'aventure architecturale, je prendrai un exemple dans un autre registre que je connais un peu mieux, celui de la photographie. Selon l'hypothèse de Wilhelm Flusser l'immense majorité des images photographiques actuelles ne traduisent plus ni le choix ni la vision du sujet photographique mais le simple déploiement de virtualité technique de l'appareil. C'est la machine qui commande, qui veut épuiser ses possibilités. L'homme n'est que l'opérateur technique du programme. Le virtuel c'est cela. C'est l'épuisement de toutes les virtualités techniques de l'appareil. On peut étendre cette analyse à l'ordinateur et à l'intelligence artificielle où la pensée n'est la plupart du temps qu'une combinatoire du logiciel, l'opération virtuelle et infinie de la machine. Tout ce qui passe ainsi par la technique et par l'immense possibilité de diversification de la technique ouvre sur une écriture automatique du monde et il en de même de l'architecture livrée à toute ses possibilités techniques. Et je ne parle pas seulement des matériaux et de la construction mais en termes de formes. De même que toutes les images sont

architectural forms can be brought up to date from a virtual stock whether in or out of order. The result is that architecture no longer refers back to some truth, to some originality, but merely to the availability of techniques, forms and materials. The truth manifested is no longer that of objective conditions and even less that of the subjective will of the architect but simply that of the machine, of its technical possibilities and its operation. We may still choose to call this architecture but it is not certain that that is what it is. Let us take, for example, the Guggenheim Museum in Bilbao, the virtual object *par excellence*, the prototype of virtual architecture designed on computer using elements or combinative modules, just as a thousand similar museums could be built by a simple change of software or calculation tables. Its relation to its contents – the collection and works of art – is totally virtual. It symbolises only the performance and the setting of an applied mental working or technology – not just any old one I admit – and the object itself is miraculous but it is an experimental miracle on a par with the biogenetic exploration taking place elsewhere; and it, too, will lead to a multitude of clones and chimeras. The Guggenheim is a spatial chimera, the fruit of intrigues that have taken over from architectural form itself. It is in fact a "ready made." Technology and equipment are turning everything into "ready mades." All the elements that will be combined are there at the outset and they need only a stage, like most post-modern forms. Duchamps did it with his bottle stand, with a real object that he turned into a virtual object by simply moving it. Today we do this with computer sequences and programmes, but it's the same thing. We take them as they are and put them in an architectural setting where they eventually become works of art. And on the subject of art we can ask ourselves, "What is this "acting out" of Duchamps that consists of transposing any object into the sphere of art by simply moving it, an aesthetic moving that puts an end to aesthetics but which leads to an aesthetic generalisation? This revolution of the "ready made," which consists in taking real objects, the real world, as a programme set in advance for an

automatic aesthetic operation and which provides an infinite perspective since all objects can enter into this virtual performance – does this radical intervention that occurred in the field of art and painting have its equivalent in architecture? Is there the same sort of break in the history of architecture, a sudden implosion, a brutal event in the sublime meaning of aesthetics with the result that everything that happened from then on in the field of art no longer had the same meaning? All that occurs, to some extent, beyond the end on the basis of the disappearance of art as such. And I should like to ask the same question with regard to architecture. Is there something that has occurred in the history of architecture that has had the result that everything that has occurred since has done so on the basis of the disappearance of architecture as such, I mean as history, as configuration, as the symbolic configuration of society. I find this an attractive hypothesis and, as something beyond their discipline, it should seduce even architects.

This question can be asked in politics also. Doesn't all that occurs on the so-called political scene occur on the basis of the disappearance of politics and the political will as such? This can be summed up as a more general hypothesis: does everything that occurs today in any field take place on the basis of the disappearance of the real and in the realm of the virtual? This hypothesis is not without hope. Perhaps it is much more interesting to see what happens beyond the end rather than purely and simply prolonging the history of art. It makes all that happens after this disappearance both original and exceptional. Everything can appear again, provided there is a hypothesis of disappearance. I like the radicality of this hypothesis because I should like architecture, the architectural object, to remain something exceptional and not be corrupted by all that lies in wait for us today on all sides in the virtual reality of architecture. And we are there. Architecture today is devoted to a great extent to culture, to communication, that is to the virtual aestheticisation of the whole of society. It serves as a museum for the conditioning of that social form

possibles à partir de l'appareil photographique, qui ne demande qu'à fonctionner, qui exige de fonctionner. Ainsi toutes les formes architecturales peuvent être réactualisées à partir d'un stock virtuel dans l'ordre ou dans le désordre. Du coup l'architecture ne renvoie plus à une quelconque vérité, à une quelconque originalité, mais à la simple disponibilité de techniques, de formes et de matériaux. La vérité qu'elle émet n'est même plus celle des conditions objectives, encore moins celle d'une volonté subjective de l'architecte, mais tout simplement celle de l'appareil, des dispositifs techniques et de son fonctionnement. On peut encore choisir d'appeler ça de l'architecture, mais rien n'est moins sûr. Prenons par exemple le musée Guggenheim de Bilbao. Voilà un objet virtuel par excellence, le prototype d'une architecture virtuelle composé sur ordinateur à partir d'éléments ou de modules combinatoires tels qu'un millier de musées semblables, semblables mais différents bien sûr, peuvent être construits en changeant simplement de logiciel ou de table de calcul. Sa relation même à son contenu, collection et oeuvres d'art est tout à fait virtuelle. Il ne symbolise que la performance et la mise en scène

d'une machinerie, une technologie mentale appliquée – pas n'importe lesquelles je reconnais, et l'objet lui est prodigieux – mais c'est un prodige expérimental comparable à l'exploration biogénétique, qui a lieu ailleurs et qui va donner lieu à des tas de clones et de chimères. Le Guggenheim est une chimère spatiale, fruit d'une machination qui a pris le pas sur la forme architecturale elle-même. En fait, c'est un "ready made" et c'est vrai qu'à travers la technique et l'appareillage, tout devient "ready made." Tous les éléments qui vont se combiner sont là d'abord et il n'est que de les remettre en scène comme la plupart des formes postmodernes. Duchamps faisait ça avec son porte-bouteilles, avec un objet réel dont il faisait un objet virtuel par simple déplacement. Aujourd'hui on fait cela avec des séquences et des programmes informatiques mais c'est la même chose. On les prend tels quels et on les porte sur la scène architecturale où ils deviennent éventuellement des oeuvres d'art. Justement à propos d'art on peut se poser la question: Est-ce que cette espèce d'"acting out" de Duchamps, qui consiste à transposer n'importe quel objet dans la sphère de l'art par simple

déplacement, déplacement esthétique qui met fin à l'esthétique mais qui ouvre sur une esthétique généralisée, comment c'est? – si cette révolution du "ready made" qui consiste à prendre des objets réels, le monde réel, comme programme donné d'avance pour une opération esthétique automatique et qui ouvre sur une perspective infinie puisque tous les objets sont susceptibles d'entrer dans cette performance virtuelle; est-ce que cette intervention radicale, qui a eu lieu dans la domaine de l'art et de la peinture, a son équivalent quelque part dans la sphère architecturale? Est-ce qu'il y a une rupture comme celle-là dans l'histoire de l'architecture? Quelque chose comme une implosion soudaine, un événement brutal du sens sublime de l'esthétique tel que tout ce qui advient dès lors dans le domaine de l'art n'aura plus jamais le même sens. Tout adviendra en quelque sorte au-delà de la fin sur la base d'une disparition de l'art en tant que tel. Et j'aimerais poser la même question quant à l'architecture. Est-ce que quelque chose n'a pas eu lieu en architecture tel que tout ce qui s'y fait depuis ait lieu sur la base d'une disparition de l'architecture en tant que telle, je veux dire en tant

qu'histoire, en tant que configuration, configuration symbolique d'une société. Je trouve cette hypothèse séduisante et elle devrait séduire même les architectes, celle d'un au-delà de leur discipline.

La question se pose pour le politique aussi. Est-ce que tout ce qui a lieu aujourd'hui sur la scène soi-disant politique n'a pas lieu sur la base d'une disparition du politique et de la volonté politique en tant que telle? Et cela se résume dans l'hypothèse la plus générale, est-ce que tout ce qui a lieu aujourd'hui dans tous les domaines n'a pas lieu sur la base d'une disparition du réel, tout simplement dans le virtuel? Cette hypothèse n'est pas désespérée du tout. Il est peut-être même beaucoup plus passionnant de voir ce qui se passe au-delà de la fin que de prolonger purement et simplement l'histoire de l'art. Cela donne à tout ce qui peut advenir au-delà de cette disparition un caractère original et exceptionnel. Tout peut apparaître encore à condition de faire l'hypothèse de la disparition. J'aime la radicalité de cette hypothèse parce que j'aimerais que l'architecture, que l'objet architectural, reste quelque chose d'exceptionnel et ne s'abîme pas dans tout ce qui nous guette aujourd'hui de toute part dans la

called culture, of immaterial needs that have no definition other than their inscription in innumerable cultural buildings. When people are not made into museum pieces where they stand in museums, where they become the virtual actors of their own life, a kind of living "ready mades" transformed into fossils, they are set down in or drawn towards the vast more or less interactive warehouses that are the commercial cultural centres of the whole world, or towards places of circulation and transit, virtual spaces so rightly dubbed "vanishing places." In Osaka, in Japan, a memorial to twenty-first century communication has already been built.

Today architecture is the slave of all these functions of circulation, information, communication and culture. There is here a gigantic functionalism that is no longer that of a mechanical world, a world of organic needs, of real social relations, but a functionalism of the virtual, that is most often attached to useless function where architecture itself risks becoming a useless function. The risk is the proliferation throughout the world of an architecture of clones and more or less identical cloned buildings, that are transparent, interactive, mobile, ludic, in the image of virtual networks and virtual reality, in which the whole of society devotes itself to the comedy of culture, the comedy of communication, the comedy of the virtual, just as it devotes itself to the comedy of politics and finally also to the comedy of art and architecture.

> **There is here a gigantic functionalism ... of the virtual, that is most often attached to useless function where architecture itself risks becoming a useless function.**

Can there be an architecture of real time, an architecture of flux and networks, an architecture of absolute or virtual visibility, of what is operational, of transparency; a polymorphic architecture with a variable purpose. A delightful small museum built in Nice by Kenzo Tange remained empty for several years with no contents but it could be perceived as a museum of the void. It could just as easily have become a craft centre or anything else. Most of today's collective buildings are too large and give an impression of emptiness rather than of space; and the works and the people that circulate there are themselves like virtual objects. There seems to be no necessity for their presence, a sort of empty functionality, a functionality of useless space. I am thinking especially of the Centro Cultural de Belém in Lisbon, France's Grande Bibliothèque, etc.

Today everything is caught up in this metastasis of culture, which is not that of architecture. It is very difficult today to distinguish what is secret in a building – that individuality I spoke of and which I do not think has really disappeared for I believe it to be indestructible – from what has been devoured by culture, a culture embracing all existing technologies and which is itself a mental technology influenced by every available model. Obviously, the architect is subject to urban and geographical constraints, the constraints of the commission, financial constraints, but there are above all models, those in the head of the developer or the client but also those that circulate in the architectural journals and that are part of the history of architectural forms. All these models impose a certain number of parameters, which means that very often the result is a collage of objects which constitutes the compromise that will pose the least problems. The drama of contemporary architecture is this endless cloning of the same type of housing all over the world based on the parameters of functionality or on the pretext of remaining faithful to a culture in terms of typical or picturesque architecture, the final result being an architectural object that not only fails to go beyond its own project but no longer goes beyond its own programme.

Has architecture lost its shadow like Chamasse's hero Peter Schlemihl who sold his name to the Devil? Once it has become transparent to all available models, it will no longer do anything but repeat itself ad infinitum, or model itself on all the nuances of a programmed code, the sort of code that declines its generic stock of conventional forms just like a genetic code.

Looking again at the twin towers of the World Trade Center, I do not deny the architectural event that it constitutes

and that I find admirable. It can be said that one is the shadow of the other, the exact replica. But, in fact, the shadow is no longer there; it has become a clone. The role of otherness, of secrecy and mystery of which the shadow is the metaphor has disappeared leaving a genetic copy of the same, where the loss of the shadow signifies the disappearance of the sun, without which, as we know, things would not be what they are. And, effectively, in our virtual universe, our universe of clones, our universe without shadows, things are only what they are. And they are what they are in innumerable copies, multiplying freely, for to some extent the shadow is the measure of the being, it sets its limits and is what prevents it from reproducing itself ad infinitum.

But all hope is not lost. Even if architecture is no longer the invention of a world, we can hope that it is something more than the invention of its more or less kitsch or designer self, something more than a geological layer of concrete, a new sedimentation of the quaternary that covers the whole planet.

The field of photography offers the possibility of wresting some exceptional images by bypassing the automatic use of the camera which has infinite technical potential and a tendency to engender a flow of uncontrollable images. As we know, automatic writing is never truly automatic and there is always the chance of a material accident or an unforeseen sequence. In the visual profusion of images that overwhelm us there is still the chance of recreating the original, primitive setting of the image. In a certain sense, all images retain something of the wild and fantastic, and our intuition can find this punctum (to use Barthes' word), this secret of the image, provided that we take it literally. But it is up to us to want such literalness. It is up to us to make secret this secret, to ensure the failure of the general aesthetisation and the mental technology of culture. And so it is conceivable that in architecture too we can start from the genius loci, from the pleasure of the place, while taking into account things that are often in the realm of change, to invent other strategies and other settings; to work against the universal cloning of human beings, of

places, of buildings and against the irruption of a universal reality, what I shall call a poetic transfer of situation or a poetic situation of transfer. Towards a poetic architecture, a dramatic architecture, a literal architecture, a radical architecture, of which, of course, we all dream. No truth, no aesthetic value, nothing based on the function, the meaning, the project or the programme but everything in its literalness. One more example. The Pompidou Centre again. What is the origin of the Pompidou? Does it speak of art, of aesthetics, of culture? No. It speaks of circulation, of stocks, of flows of individuals, objects and signs. And the architecture of the Pompidou states this very clearly. Literally, it is an object born out of an obscure disaster. More precisely, from the obscure disaster of culture. What is fantastic, even if it is involuntary, is that it reveals both culture itself, and to what it has succumbed. What it is succumbing to more and more is perfusion, suffusion, to the confusion of all signs. This is also true of the World Trade Center. The miracle is that it provides a fantastic spectacle of the city, of verticality at its most radical, and is at the same time a flagrant model of what the city is succumbing to; it is the symbol of what the city died of as a historical form. What makes this architecture so powerful, is that it is at the same time a form of extreme anticipation and retrospective nostalgia for a lost object.

And so these were just a few fragments of the primal arena of architecture as seen through the imagination of an outsider. You can interpret them literally and in every sense, as Rimbaud put it; one of the possible meanings being that there still exists beyond all illusion or disillusion a future for architecture in which I believe, even if that future of architecture is not necessarily architectural. There is a future for architecture for the simple reason that we have not yet invented the building, the architectural object that will put an end to all the rest, that will put an end to space itself; nor have we invented the city that will put an end to all cities, nor the thought that will put an end to all thought. That is our fundamental dream. But until it is achieved, there is still hope.

---

du tout à l'événement architecturale qu'elles constituent que je trouve admirable. On pourrait dire que l'une est l'ombre de l'autre, la réplique exacte. Mais, précisément, l'ombre n'est plus là; elle est devenue clone. La part d'altérité, de secret, de mystère dont l'ombre est la métaphore a disparu laissant place à une copie génétique du même où la perte de l'ombre signifie la disparition du soleil, sans lequel, comme on sait, les choses ne seraient que ce qu'elles sont. Et, effectivement, dans notre univers virtuel, notre univers de clones, notre univers sans ombre, les choses ne sont que ce qu'elles sont. Elles le sont même à d'innombrables exemplaires multipliant toute liberté puisque l'ombre était en quelque sorte la mesure de l'être, sa limite singulière, ce qui lui évitait de se reproduire à l'infini.

J'ai cependant quelque espoir. Si l'architecture n'est plus l'invention d'un monde, on peut espérer quelle soit autre chose qu'une répétition d'elle-même plus ou moins kitsch ou design, autre chose qu'une couche géologique de béton, une nouvelle sédimentation de l'époque du quaternaire appliquée à toute la planète.

Je reviens à la photographie. Il y a dans la domaine de la photographie une possibilité

d'arracher à l'automaticité de l'appareil, dont les potentialités techniques sont infinies, et dont la tendance est d'engendrer un flux incoercible d'images, d'arracher à cela quelques images exceptionnelles. Comme on sait, l'écriture automatique n'est jamais vraiment automatique et il y a toujours la chance du hasard objectif ou d'enchaînement imprévisible. Dans la profusion visuelle d'images qui nous submerge il y a encore une chance de recréer une scène primitive sauvage de l'image. Dans un certain sens n'importe quelle image a gardé quelque chose de sauvage et de fantastique et l'intuition peut retrouver ce punctum, comme dirait Barthes, ce secret de l'image à condition de la prendre dans sa littéralité. Et cette littéralité c'est à nous de la vouloir. Ce secret c'est à nous de le secréter de faire échec à cette esthétation générale et à cette technologie mentale de la culture. Ainsi on peut penser que dans l'architecture aussi on peut à partir du génie du lieu, à partir du plaisir du lieu peut-être, et en tenant compte de choses qui sont souvent de l'ordre du hasard, inventer d'autres stratégies, d'autres dramaturgies, d'opérer contre ce clonage universel des hommes, des lieux, des édifices,

contre cette irruption d'une réalité virtuelle universelle, ce que j'appellerai un transfert poétique de situation ou une situation poétique de transfert, vers une architecture poétique, une architecture dramatique, une architecture littérale, une architecture radicale, dont nous continuons tous de rêver, bien entendu. Pas de vérité là-dedans, pas de valeur esthétique, transparente, rien dans la fonction, rien dans la signification, rien dans le projet, rien dans le programme, tout est dans la littéralité.

Un exemple encore. Beaubourg de nouveau. Ca parle de quoi Beaubourg? Ca parle d'art, d'esthétique, de culture? Non. Ca parle de circulation, de stockage, de flux que ce soit d'individus, d'objets et de signes. Et cela, l'architecture de Beaubourg le dit très bien. Littéralement c'est un objet issu d'un désastre obscur. Du désastre obscur de la culture précisément. Ce qui est fantastique, même si c'est involontaire c'est que ça donne à voir en même temps la culture et ce à quoi a succombé la culture. Ce à quoi elle succombe de plus en plus, à la perfusion, à la suffusion, à la confusion de tous les signes. Même chose pour le World Trade

Center. Son miracle est de donner simultanément un spectacle fantastique de la ville, de la verticalité dans son expression la plus radicale et le modèle de symbole flagrant de ce à quoi succombe la ville, de ce à quoi elle a succombé et elle est morte comme forme historique. C'est ce qui fait la puissance d'une telle architecture, elle est à la fois une forme d'anticipation extrême et de nostalgie rétrospective d'un objet perdu.

Voilà donc quelques fragments d'une scène primitive de l'architecture vue par l'imagination d'un sauvage. Vous pouvez les interpréter littéralement et dans tous les sens, comme disait Rimbaud, un des sens possible étant qu'il existe encore au-delà de toute illusion ou désillusion un futur de l'architecture auquel je crois, même si ce futur de l'architecture n'est pas forcément architectural. Il y a un futur de l'architecture pour la simple raison qu'on n'a pas encore inventé l'édifice, l'objet architectural qui mettrait fin à tous les autres, qui mettrait fin à l'espace lui-même, ni la ville qui mettrait fin à toutes les villes, ni la pensée qui mettrait fin à toutes les pensées. Or, c'est bien là notre rêve fondamental. Tant qu'il n'est pas réalisé il y a encore de l'espoir.

Kenneth Frampton

Megaform as Urban Landscape

Since 1961 when the French geographer Jean Gottmann first employed the term megalopolis to allude to the north-eastern seaboard of the United States, the world population has become increasingly dense with the result that most of us now live in some form of continuous urbanized region. One of the paradoxical consequences of this population shift is that today we are largely unable to project urban form with any degree of confidence, neither as a *tabula rasa* operation nor as a piecemeal aggregation to be achieved through such devices as zoning codes maintained over a long period of time. The constant expansion of the autoroute infrastructure throughout the world continues to open up increasing tracts of former agricultural land to suburban subdivision. Despite this endless suburbanized development throughout the world and most particularly in North America, there remains the occasional capital city where some kind of urban planning process is still being significantly maintained such as Helsinki or the recent refurbishing of Barcelona, which is yet another example of an exception to the megalopolitan norm.

In the main, however, the urban future tends to be projected largely in terms of remedial operations as these may be applied to existing urban cores or, with less certainty, to selected parts of the megalopolis. Meanwhile, the urbanized region continues to consolidate its hold over vast areas of land as in the Randstadt in the Netherlands or the Tokyo-Hokkaido corridor in Japan. These urbanized regions are subject to sporadic waves of urban expansion that either escalate out of control or enter into periods of stagnation. It is a predicament that confronts the urbanist with an all but impossible task, one in which civic intervention has to be capable not only of sustaining a sense of place but also of serving as an effective catalyst for the further development of the region.

Owing to the dissolution of the city as a bounded domain, dating from the mid-nineteenth century, architects have long since been aware that any contribution they might make to the urban form would of necessity be extremely limited. This resignation is already implicit in Camillo Sitte's remedial urban strategy of 1889. In his book, *City Planning according to Artistic Principles*, he attempted to respond to the "space-endlessness" of the Viennese Ringstrasse by recommending the redefinition of the Ring in terms of bounded form. Sitte was evidently disturbed by the fact that the main monuments of the Ring had been built as free-standing objects and he recommended enclosing them with built fabric in order to establish relationships similar to those that had once existed in the medieval city, such as that between the *parvis* and the *cathedral*.

Inspired by Sitte's revisionism, I have coined the term *megaform* in order to refer to the form-giving potential of certain kinds of horizontal urban fabric capable of effecting

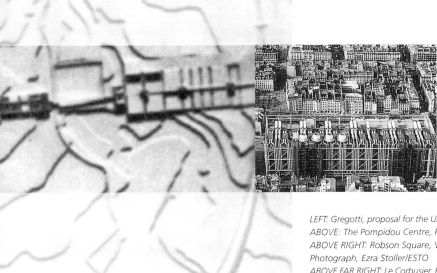

LEFT: Gregotti, proposal for the University of Calabria
ABOVE: The Pompidou Centre, Paris
ABOVE RIGHT: Robson Square, Vancouver
Photograph, Ezra Stoller/ESTO
ABOVE FAR RIGHT: Le Corbusier, Plan Orbus for Algiers

some kind of topographic transformation in the megalopolitan landscape. It has to be admitted at the outset that this term may read as being synonymous with the term megastructure, as this was first coined in the 1960s. In my view, the two terms may be differentiated from one another in terms of the relative continuity of their form. Thus, while a megaform may incorporate a megastructure, a megastructure is not necessarily a megaform.

One may illustrate this distinction by comparing the Centre Pompidou in Paris, which is surely a megastructure, to Arthur Erickson's Robson Square development in Vancouver, which is ultimately a megaform. This is largely due to the way in which its continuously stepped layered form serves to modulate and unify the existing urban fabric of downtown Vancouver. This particular example also happens to have been enriched by an exceptionally fertile collaboration between its architect, Erickson, and the landscape architect, Cornelia Oberlander.

It seems that our capacity to imagine megaforms may well have originated with our first experiences of the world as seen from the air. This, on his own admission, was the catalyst behind Le Corbusier's Plan Obus for Algiers of 1931 that was directly inspired by the volcanic topography of Rio de Janeiro which he first surveyed from the air in 1929. This sweeping panorama led him to imagine a continuous urban form in

which one could no longer discriminate between the building and the landscape. A corollary to this topographic approach was to treat the built fabric as a form of artificial ground, upon which and within which the occupant would be free to build in whatever way he saw fit. Hence, while postulating the continuity of the megaform, Le Corbusier left its interstitial fabric open and accessible to popular taste. In its failure to conform to any received urban model, the Plan Obus was hardly a feasible proposal from either a productive or a cultural standpoint. It was totally removed, let us say, from Joseph Stubben's codification of regularized urban space as this had been set forth in his book *Die Stadtebau* of 1890. Nor did it owe anything to the perimeter block type, as this would be applied to urban extensions from around 1890 to 1924 and of which Berlage's Amsterdam South plan of 1915 is a prime example. At the same time neither did it conform to the Zeilenbau row house model which was adopted in the Weimar Republic and elsewhere from around 1924 onwards.

Despite the endless suburbanized development throughout the world there remains the occasional capital city where some kind of urban planning process is still being significantly maintained

For our purposes, the megaform may be defined as the displaying of the following characteristics: 1) A large form extending horizontally rather than vertically. 2) A complex form which, unlike the megastructure, is not necessarily articulated into a series of structural and mechanical subsets as we find for example in the Centre Pompidou. 3) A form

capable of inflecting the existing urban landscape as found because of its strong topographical character. 4) A form that is not freestanding but rather insinuates itself as a continuation of the surrounding topography. And last but not least 5) A form that is oriented towards a densification of the urban fabric.

Beyond the dense historical core, a megaform may be identified as an urban nexus set within the "space-endlessness" of the megalopolis. Henri Ciriani's concept of *une pièce urbaine* as first formulated in his so called Barre à Marne or Noissy I complex, realized in Marne la Vallée in 1980, certainly seems to have been conceived along these lines and something similar may also be claimed for Rafael Moneo and Manuel de Sola Morales's L'Illa Block as realized in Barcelona in 1997.

The idea of megaform is also implicit as a strategy in Vittorio Gregotti's concept of the anthrogeographic landscape as this is set forth in his book *Il territorio di architettura* of 1966. Drawing on the work of the German geographer Friedrich Ratzel, who first coined the term anthrogeographic, Gregotti was able to evolve a territorial approach to urban design that, among his Neo-Rationalist colleagues, put him in a class apart.

Architects can only intervene urbanistically in an increasingly remedial manner and one effective instrument for this is the large building programme that might be rendered as a megaform While not opposing the Neo-Rationalist project of reconstructing the neo-classical European city along traditional, typological lines as hypothesized by Aldo Rossi, Léon Krier et al., Gregotti was more intent on responding to the challenge of the megalopolis at a regional scale – at a scale that was closer to that of Le Corbusier's Plan Obus which he recognized as a precedent. Hence his Zen housing scheme for Palermo of 1965 may be seen as combining the Zeilenbau pattern of Weimar with the perimeter block approach of Amsterdam. His scheme for the University of Florence designed two years later was much more territorial with its long blocks running out into the agrarian landscape. This approach took on an even more expansive geographic dimension in his proposal for the University of Calabria of 1973, where the "spine" of the university cuts across five hills

between a take-off from the regional autoroute and a railroad station. Partially realized, this infrastructure remains a canonical piece in as much as it is both ordered and yet open to random development. Blocks were designed to be freely attached to the spine without compromising its ability to impinge on the landscape at a panoramic scale.

If one looks for the origin of the megaform in the history of the Modern Movement one tends to find it in Northern Europe rather than the Mediterranean. One first encounters it in Bruno Taut's concept of the "city crown" as it appears in his book *Die Stadtkrone* of 1919. This becomes manifest in the ensuing decade in the German cult of the big building form as it appears in the work of a number of Expressionist architects of the 1920s, including such figures as Hans Scharoun, Hugo Häring, Fritz Höger and Hans Poelzig. One finds in these architects a predisposition for creating large, dynamic urban entities in opposition to the dematerialized spatial dynamics of the twentieth century avant-garde. One thinks of such canonical works as Hans Poelzig's House of Friendship projected for Istanbul in 1916, Hugo Häring's Gut Garkau of 1924, Fritz Höger's Chilehaus in Hamburg of 1925 and Hans Scharoun's Breslau Werkbund exhibition building of 1929. In the case of Poelzig's Istanbul project, one is struck by the way in which the distant silhouette of the building rises diagonally out of the horizontal profile of the city, so that it assumes the form of an artificial escarpment, replete with hanging gardens.

There were of course other German architects in this period who were to embrace a similar topographic strategy – above all Reich, whose project for Alexanderplatz, Berlin of 1927 rises out of the existing street fabric like a dynamic force. The megaform seems to be an embryonic presence in almost all of Mendelsohn's work from his diminutive Einstein Tower in Potsdam of 1920 to his commercial centre for Haifa of 1924 and his heroic Hadassah Hospital projected for Mount Scorpus in 1935. The megaform was also evident in the work of Lois Welzenbacher, above all in his competition entry for Berlin Hazelhorst housing of 1928.

Among Scandinavian architects, the one who lies closest to this German tradition is Alvar Aalto, as is most evident perhaps from his Baker Dormitory, completed on the edge of the Charles River in Cambridge, Massachusetts in 1944. However, a perennial topographic syndrome is manifest in Aalto's work throughout his mature career, from the "tented-mountain" he projected for the Vogelweidplatz Sports Centre in Vienna in 1953 to the Pensions Institute realized in Helsinki in 1956. A similar stress upon megaform is also evident in his proposal of the mid-sixties for a new cultural district in the Tooloo area of Helsinki wherein a terraced autoroute system transforms the morphology of the centre, serving as a topographic link and a dynamic binder between a series of cultural buildings lining the lake and the major rail head entering the city.

Something approaching a megaform strategy may also be found in the work of Team X, above all perhaps in Jacob Bakema's Bochum University proposal of 1962, his plan for Tel Aviv of 1963 and his Pampas Plan for Rotterdam of 1965. Both Bakema and the British architects Alison and Peter Smithson seem to have regarded the autoroute infrastructure as the sole element which could be depended upon when projecting the future of urban form. This accounts for the Smithsons' Berlin Haupstadt Competition entry of 1958. The megaform theme also plays a role in the work of Ralph Erskine, above all in his Svappavaara proposal for Lapland of 1963 and in his later Byker Wall housing complex completed in 1981 at Newcastle, England.

To my knowledge the term megaform as opposed to megastructure is first used rather coincidentally by Fumihiko Maki and Masato Ohtaka in their essay "Some Thoughts on Collective Form" of 1965. They introduce the term when writing an appreciation of Kenzo Tange's Tokyo Bay Project of 1960 to the effect that:

"One of the most interesting developments of the megaform has been suggested by Kenzo Tange in connection with the Tokyo Bay Project. He presents a proposal for a mass-human scale form which includes a megaform and discrete, rapidly changing, functional units which fit within the larger framework. He reasons that short-lived items are becoming more and more short-lived and the cycle of change is shrinking at a corresponding rate. On the other hand, the accumulation of capital has made it possible to build in large scale operations. . ."

For Maki and Ohtaka, the megaform concept depended upon the idea that change would occur less rapidly in some realms than others. On this basis, they introduced the idea of group form, with the notion that a podium may be inserted into an urban fabric in order to provide for a long term stability while the structures on its surface would be subject to a faster cycle of change and replacement. This concept was exemplified at the time in their joint proposal for the Shinjuku area of Tokyo in which they proposed building a podium above the Shinjuku transit terminal, while at the same time introducing new shopping facilities at grade with parking beneath and rather random, medium-rise offices and residential structures above. Maki's subsequent work has contributed to the theme of the megaform. Like the "city-crown" projects of Jørn Utzon, it is a form that generally manifests itself at two levels, so that while it emphasizes the importance of the podium/earthwork, almost as a precondition, it also depends on the roofwork as an element that is essential to the hill-like character of the final form, as we find this in Bruno Taut's vision of the "city-crown." This double paradigm of earthwork/roofwork first fully emerges in Maki's Fujisawa Gymnasium of 1980 and reappears in his Tokyo Metropolitan Gymnasium of 1985 and in his Makahari Convention Centre, Chiba of 1989.

Late capitalism seems reluctant to commit itself to any form of land settlement that would be consistent with the production of civic form

The Ticinese Neo-Rationalist architects of the early seventies also gravitated towards the megaform. This is particularly true for the urban projects designed by Mario Botta and Luigi Snozzi, above all their "viaduct" block proposal for a new

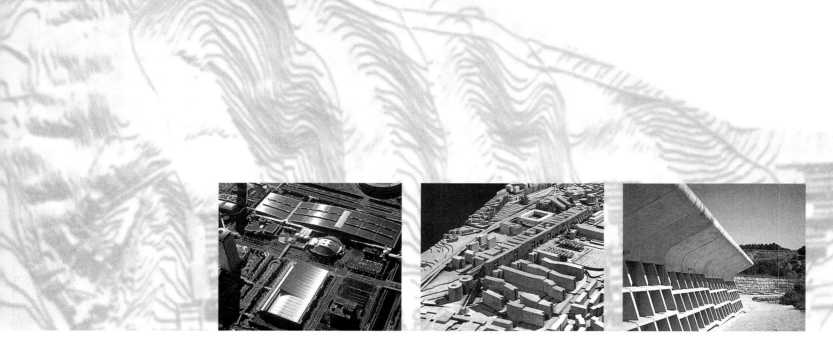

administration centre in Perugia of 1977 and their air rights project for the Zurich rail terminal of 1981. Perugia is particularly interesting in this regard for, like the afore-mentioned L'Illa Block in Barcelona, it posited a long orthog-onal structure containing a flexible space-form within. One end of this "viaduct" was fed by parking silos that were con-nected to the hill town of Perugia by a *teleferico*.

Adhering to a similar format the project for the Zurich term-inus designed by Botta and Snozzi not only denoted the line of the buried Sihl River, but also provided new ticketing facilities while at the same time being connected to a large multi-storey parking garage built over the rail tracks entering the station. This proposal would have revitalized the rail network by linking it directly to the road infrastructure, while at the same time maintaining the old terminus and restoring a trace of the original topography, namely, a tributary to the Limmet that was covered over by the railhead in the nine-teenth century.

Large building forms are particularly evident at an urban scale in the work of Rafael Moneo, from his Roman Museum erected in Merida in 1986 to his Atocha Station completed in Madrid in 1992 and his recent proposal for two auditoria on a podium overlooking the seafront in San Sebastian. In each instance, the morphology of the structure gives a particular inflection to the surrounding topography. In Madrid, the hypostyle of the new high-speed train shed slides into the rear of the old station in such a way as to render the overall form legible over a much wider area. Megaforms are also in evidence in the work of a number of Catalan architects including Esteven Bonell and Francesc Rius, whose Velodrome d'Horta built in the Vall d'Hebron neighbourhood of Barcelona in 1986 establishes a particularly powerful landmark in the midst of urban chaos. Here is the condition of a bounding ring of auxiliary spaces enclosing the elliptical form of the bicycle track within.

> **The origin of architecture is not the primitive hut, but the marking of ground, to establish a cosmic order around the surrounding chaos of nature**
>
> *Vittorio Gregotti*

In his archery building for the 1992 Barcelona Olympics, the Catalan architect Enric Miralles designed a building which is extremely sensitive to the landscape and which becomes the landscape. In his scheme for the Igualada Cemetery, realized in a disused quarry and dating from the same year, it is difficult to say whether this is a building, a series of buildings, the city of the dead or the landscape. It is so much a landscape form that it is difficult to say where landscape ends and building begins. Miralles has always striven to give his architecture a topograph-ic character, one that either animates a flat site or fuses it with pre-existing heavily contoured form. Clearly landform as a radical reshaping of the ground may be used to impart shape to a terrain that would otherwise be totally formless.

One may object that the megaform approach gives sufficient attention to the transport infrastructure or, conversely, that the physical form of the city is of little consequence in a telematic age. Alternatively, one may claim that urban culture in a classical sense can only be reconstituted typologically or, conversely, that the traditional context of the historical city is no longer pertinent. Each of these polarized positions seems to be somewhat evasive to the extent that they fail to confront the responsibility of giving an identifiable shape or inflection to the later modern megalopolis.

Given the ruthless forms of motopian development that are currently transforming vast tracts of the Asian continent, we are again reminded that cities can no longer be realized as coherent entities according to the dictates of some master plan, nor can they always be developed in culturally sig-nificant ways on an incremental basis. While this last may have always been the case, what has changed dramatically in the last fifty years is the rate of technological change and the rapacity of development, occurring at a speed and scale which totally outstrips anything that urbanized society had experienced in the past. In addition to this, we may note that in many parts of the world the land is no longer significantly productive, that is to say, it is no longer used as a site for

OPPOSITE LEFT: Maki and Ohtaka, Shinjuku transit
terminal. Photograph, Satoru Mishima
OPPOSITE CENTRE: Mario Botta and Luigi Snozzi,
"viaduct" block proposal for a new administration
centre, Perugia
OPPOSITE RIGHT: Enric Miralles, Igualada Cemetery
BELOW: Esteven Bonell and Francesc Rius,
Velodrome d'Horta, Barcelona

either agricultural or industrial production. Instead there is a noticeable tendency to reduce the ground itself to a commodity through the interrelated processes of tourism, land speculation and the global expansion of the service industry. Under these conditions, late capitalism seems reluctant to commit itself to any form of land settlement that would be consistent with the production of coherent civic form.

Thus we may conclude that architects can only intervene urbanistically in an increasingly remedial manner and that one effective instrument for this is the large building programme that may be rendered as a megaform – as an element which due to its size, content and direction has the capacity to inflect the surrounding landscape and give it a particular orientation and identity. I believe that such forms are capable of returning us to a time when the prime object of architecture was not the proliferation of freestanding objects but rather the marking of ground. As Vittorio Gregotti remarked, the origin of architecture resides in the creation of a microcosmos. He puts it: "Before transforming a support into a column, a roof into a tympanum, before placing stone on stone, man placed the stone on the ground to recognize a site in the midst of an unknown universe; in order to take account of it and modify it. . ."

I have attempted to trace the recurrence of the megaform as a unifying environmental trope in twentieth century architecture and civic design in an effort to suggest that it may be one of the only formal legacies that remain available for the realistic mediation of the random megalopolis as an iterated form. Clearly not all the examples I have cited are pitched at the same scale or at an equal level of abstraction nor do they possess the same potential feasibility. Despite these variations, they all tend to blur in different ways the conventional differentiation between architecture and landscape. Like canals, railway cuttings, autoroutes, dykes and other artificial earthworks, they all have the potential of gathering up the contingent landscape around them by virtue

of their anthrogeographic status, so much so that they may, at some juncture, appear to merge with the ground or alternatively to acquire, through their topographic presence, the status of being a landmark.

A certain "kinetic horizontality" is almost a precondition for the emergence of such forms, and in this regard it is important to observe that free-standing high-rise structures, for all their rival potential as landmarks do not attain the same anthrogeographic status, unless they happen to be of the same height and rhythmically linked in a compelling way at grade. While this may seem to be a prescription verging on formalism, it should be evident that the arbitrary horizontal packaging of the programme, irrespective of content, is not desirable. It is essential that our horizontal megaforms serve as civic microcosms and that they function as identifiable spaces of public appearance within the universal, ever-expanding context of Melvin Webber's "non-place urban realm." Hence it is not so difficult to adumbrate the programmatic types that seem to have the potential of engendering such forms. Aside from the unlikely prospect of being able to achieve extended areas of low-rise, high-density housing, one thinks, in no particular order, of shopping malls, air terminals, transport interchanges, hospitals, hotels, sports facilities, and universities – a series of type-forms in fact that still have a certain currency, not to say urgency, within the ever-expanding domain of the megalopolis.

In an address in 1983, Vittorio Gregotti asserted that, "The origin of architecture is not the primitive hut, but the marking of ground, to establish a cosmic order around the surrounding chaos of nature." Now we have made a new nature – this technological urbanized region which is the new chaos – but as architects and urbanists we still have the same task.

Lionel March

From Digital and Beyond

The Queen's House, Inigo Jones, 1615-16. The Royal Naval Hospital, Greenwich, Sir Christopher Wren and others, 1665 onwards.

Professor Lionel March, former Rector of the Royal College of Art in London, now at UCLA, was one of the keynote speakers at the International Symposium "Greenwich 2000. Digital Creativity: Architecture. Landscape. Design" organized by the University of Greenwich. The following paper was presented on 13 January 2000 in the Chapel of St Peter and St Paul at the Old Royal Naval College.

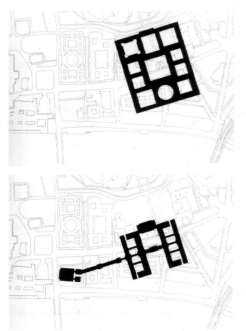

Proposals for rebuilding Whitehall, London:
TOP: Inigo Jones and John Webb, 1630-40
ABOVE: Sir Christopher Wren, 1669-85

Departure

As a student in Cambridge, three of my architectural role models were Inigo Jones, Christopher Wren and John Vanbrugh. The site of this conference could not be more appropriate for my address today. Inigo Jones and Vanbrugh inspired my early adventures in the theatre and particularly the design of stage settings for works from Sophocles to Stravinsky. In working with Sir Leslie Martin on the development of a national and government centre in Whitehall, Inigo Jones and Christopher Wren were our ghostly companions. In the official report, *Whitehall*, we reproduced the Jones and Webb plan for Whitehall, and Wren's later project. But perhaps my favourite English architecture of this period is by Nicholas Hawksmore, whose tombstone reads not 'architect,' but 'scientist.'

I shall reflect here my own interest in dissolving the conventional and popular differences between science and design while clearly distinguishing between the two. In some respects, the concept of 'computation' has been central to my life-long ambition to restore 'one culture' – the arts and sciences together as aesthetic adventures in constructive thought.

In the English language, the word 'computation' was largely used, from the fifteenth century on, in regard to calendric calculations, but in 1665 Robert Boyle applied it to his estimate of the earth's size:

The whole Earth... by the probablest computation contains above ten thousand millions of Cubick German Leagues.

In a letter written in his retirement (1711), Wren writes:

The capacity and dimensions of the new churches may be determined by a calculation.

Wren then estimates the number of parishioners in London at 400,000 'grown persons'. Fifty new churches would need to accommodate on average 2,000 persons.

The churches must be large; but... it would seem vain to make a parish-church larger, than that all who are present can both hear and see.

Wren suggests that the preacher's voice from the pulpit will be heard 50 feet in front, 30 feet to each side, and 20 feet behind:

... the new church should be at least 60 feet broad, and 90 feet long. ... These proportions may be varied ... but to build more room, than that every person may conveniently hear and see, is to create noise and confusion.

Boyle and Wren were active founders of the Royal Society dominated by the towering intellectual authority of Isaac Newton. I will argue that computation – and specifically 'digital' computation, calculation by numbers – has followed the Newtonian doctrine to this very day; a doctrine which William Blake in 1827 characterized as 'the fluxions of an atom'. Revolutionary art, Blake writes, is inimical to the Newtonian 'atom', an indivisible entity 'which does not exist'. In the same letter, he writes:

God keep me from the Divinity of Yes and No.

A contemporary of these architects, was Thomas Hobbes who was prone to think that thought was computation. It is prudent to pay attention to his 1656

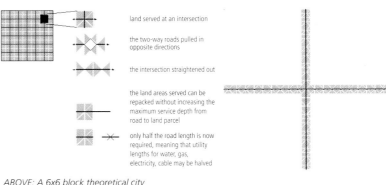

land served at an intersection

the two-way roads pulled in opposite directions

the intersection straightened out

the land areas served can be repacked without increasing the maximum service depth from road to land parcel

only half the road length is now required, meaning that utility lengths for water, gas, electricity, cable may be halved

BELOW LEFT: 6 acres of land: the land area per person on Earth today, in the year 2000
BELOW MIDDLE: 1acre of land. The land area per person proposed by Frank Lloyd Wright for Broadacre City, 1935
BELOW RIGHT: 1/21 acre of land per person. The approximate density of Hong Kong

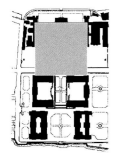
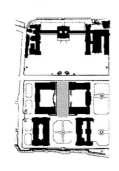
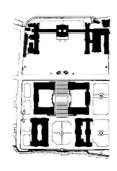

ABOVE: A 6x6 block theoretical city
ABOVE RIGHT: The linearised cruciform city serves the same land parcels with half the road length
RIGHT: The 'blob' and 'line' cities compared; the 'blob' scheme requires additional roads to connect one 'blob' with another

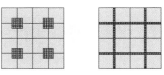

emark to which I shall return later:

We must not ... think of computation, that is ratio-ination, has place only in numbers.

shall touch on these points as I strike a path in my ddress 'From digital and beyond.'

he World in London ...

n the spirit of Boyle, I shall make a simple computation, ot of the Earth's bulk, but of the proportion of its land urface area that each of us might be said to occupy oday. The land surface area is said to be 57,000,000 lus square miles, and the population is said to have eached 6,000,000,000 persons last year. First, let us et an idea of what this population number might 'feel' ke. In the *Master Atlas of Greater London*, the pages vhich contain Greenwich form a double-spread that neasures 14 1/2 x 11 inches.[1] It covers an area which xtends from Kensington in the west to Bexley in the ast, and from Bromley in the south to Edmonton in the orth. This area equals 6,000,000,000 double-spreads f my atlas, and although there would be no elbow oom, I can stand on this double-spread! I borrow this dea from Buckminster Fuller who stood the world's opulation in his day on the island of Bermuda. It was aid that Eddington had an opening move in doctoral xaminations in physics: "How many atoms in this pin-ead?" Does the candidate have a 'fee' for what he is ealing with?

. specifically at Greenwich Hospital

et us look at Greenwich Hospital, now a campus of the niversity. The plan comes from Sir John Summerson's lassic *Architecture in Britain, 1530-1830*. The area etween the Queen's House and the William and Mary locks, framed by the wings to the Queen's House, is lose to six acres. This is the share that each of us six illion have of the Earth's land surface today – including ninhabitable deserts, mountain tops, swamps, lakes nd rivers. An extended area between the colonnades

of Queen Anne's and King Charles's blocks is one acre. This entitlement for each person would leave five-sixths of the world's land surface unoccupied. It is also the density of Frank Lloyd Wright's Broadacre City proposal of which I have broadcast and written elsewhere.

The assumption of an equal distribution is unrealistic, but distribution may complicate the computation in surprising ways. Still, to simplify, take a distribution in just two groups. Suppose that 15% of the world population has their full entitlement of six acres. What do the remaining 85% have? The answer is one-ninth of an acre, or roughly the land area that we Angelinos enjoy. Let another percentage point of the population have six acres, now what does the remaining 84% have? The answer is 1/21 of an acre, or the density of Hong Kong. A small increase in'wealth' among the few dramatically changes the decreasing resources available to the 'many.' Of course, this argument is only true for limited, non-expanding resources.

Configuring the Urban Landscape

Here I examine two possible spatial configurations of urban land: the blob and the line. My study of Frank Lloyd Wright's Broadacre City project at MIT and Harvard's Joint Center for Urban Studies, and the two years that I spent travelling 30,000 miles around the States, led me to challenge the conventional European view of city form. I first used this example in a BBC TV programme in collaboration with geographers at The Open University. On the ground, we used examples of linear developments in the Fens north of Cambridge. I conjured up a Froebelian model in which the roads were cord and the blocks were wooden tiles. Pulling on the cord changed the configuration from a 'blob' to a 'line.'

Assume a blob city with 6 x 6, or 36, square blocks. The maximum depth of service to each block is half the block size. I have arranged that one side of the two-way service road can be pulled away together with the served land area.[2]

At some point, you will see that a section of the 'blob' has been unfolded and becomes a 'line.' It will also be

seen that the blocks along the line are loosely packed, unlike the original arrangement in the 'blob.' A compact packing of urban land along the 'line' requires only half of the road length previously required in the 'blob.' This means that all the utility lengths required to serve the urban area are halved in the linear form.

To further illustrate the point imagine four 'blobs' in a landscape occupying just 1/9th of the land surface. An equal amount of land may be distributed in linear form to create an inverted landscape in which the 'blobs' become the countryside. To a designer, this is a figure-ground inversion.

In 1967, I applied this to Ebenezer Howard's scheme for garden cities and produced a retiform, or network, alternative.[3] Six years ago, on the occasion of my sixtieth birthday, Marcial Echenique commented on the prescience of this observation in a discussion of urban growth around Santiago de Chile, and around Cambridge. Of course, the computational complexity of the urban modellers far exceeds my simple kindergarten exercise. For one thing it requires the digital mapping of existing urban areas. I remember being impressed by early computerized cartographic work at Harvard, and here at Reading under Peter Hall, in the sixties. I am delighted to see that Carl Steinitz is to follow me.

Whitehall: an Architectural Case

I returned to Cambridge to be one of two principal assistants to Leslie Martin in the preparation of his plan for Whitehall which had been commissioned by the Labour Administration. As I recall, the Minister of Building and Public Works had been a demolition contractor before he rose to political power! A noble Lord, Hansard reported, put his own situation nicely:

Having myself worked for four years in a small ply-wood box erected in the corner of the Locarno Room, I can assure noble lords that the Foreign Office is about as inefficient and inconvenient a working place as could be imagined, and that the India Office is, if anything, worse.

The government's Chief Architect had just erected

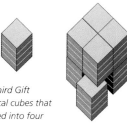

RIGHT: Froebel's Third Gift comprises 8 identical cubes that have been sectioned into four divisions to represent storeys

Sky angle 6:1
the blocks are piled high to reach 8x4=32 storeys

Sky angle 2:1
four built forms are placed on each site, each 8 storeys high

Sky angle 1:1
the blocks are distributed in court form, 4 storeys high

Sky angle 1:2
the blocks are halved in height and redistributed as shown

Sky angle 1:6
By placing the central half blocks in the previous case (sky angle 1:2) above the corners of the court, the sky angle is reduced further

BELOW: Models showing different same-volume built form distributions in the same plot. Lionel March

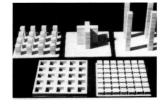

ABOVE: Proposal for rebuilding Whitehall, Sir Leslie Martin, 1965. Drawing, Lionel March

the prototype office building in Horseferry Road – three high-rise slab blocks on a podium. The question appeared to concern determining the appropriate external materials for such slab blocks if they were to be erected next to the Jones Banqueting House and the Horse Guards of William Kent. Leslie Martin took a much wider view of development than that.

I had seen Nicholas Negroponte's early experiments at MIT, and William Porter's 'Urban 5,' and proposed some computer studies. In those days architects did not have computers. We turned to Philip Dunstone, our consultant quantity surveyor. Together we constructed a mathematical model for what became known as a 'land use and built form study.' Again, I looked to Froebel's kindergarten gifts. The idea can be perfectly well demonstrated with his Third Gift, which comprises eight 1 x 1 x 1 inch cubes.

Imagine a plot 8 x 8 inches square. Place the eight cubes vertically in the centre. The 'skylight' angle between two adjacent towers is *arctan* 6, or 80°, at that time quite unacceptable to planners. Now arrange four built forms to each plot, each represented by 2 blocks. The skylight angle is now *arctan* 2, or 63°, still unacceptable. These arrangements we called pavilion forms. Now look at a courtyard form in which eight blocks are arranged around an open area, very much like a traditional Cambridge quad, or a London square. The arrangement is only one block high and the skylight angle is now *arctan* 1, or 45°, which is certainly more acceptable. The next configuration requires blocks that are half cubes.[4] The bulk of the built form can be distributed around the perimeter with a small amount placed centrally – very much the arrangement that James Stirling had used in his sadly unexecuted project with Gowan for Churchill College. Now the skylight angle is *arctan* 1/2, or 26°, which would certainly pass muster. Finally, the corners are made two blocks high by clearing the central built form. The skylight angle is now *arctan* 1/6, or 9°; barely built up at all.

This was the underlying computational notion behind the Whitehall proposal. We computed hundreds of parametrized schemes to arrive at the conclusion that the new buildings would need to be no higher than the existing fabrics, and yet would provide far more floor space on the same site. Into the equations we were able to include work by Frances Duffy who had brought to our attention German developments in *burolandschaft*, open office layouts. Christopher Alexander also worked independently from us on suitable patterns for public office entrances. The Whitehall study was surely one of the first significant uses of computers in the architectural design process.

The 'Ruskin' Model

Following the Whitehall study, I was invited by the RIBA to make a presentation at Ruskin College, Oxford. The gist of my talk was the future role of the computer in the total architectural design cycle. I remember that I was honoured by the Smithsons' presence in my audience. I showed a transparency in which the design phase interacted with the management of existing spaces on the

one hand, and the production requirements on the other. The production phase interacted with the design phase and the construction phase. The construction phase with production and management of existing fabrics; management with construction and any new design activity. The interactions were mutual and directionless. The computer acted as a central processor for all four phases.

In regard to how these four phases have developed computationally – at least in architecture, I would point to work by George Stiny, Terry Knight and colleagues including Chris Earl at the generative phase of design, to Chris Yessios and Paul Richens[5] at the production phase, and to Frances Duffy and his colleagues at the management phase. The construction phase does not appear to be represented at this conference, but my understanding is that some sophisticated systems exist, and I mention the researches in this respect of Ranko Bon at Reading. John Gero and the Key Centre group at Sydney have contributed more generally to the information technology and scientific aspects of the design process.

At the urban-scale the four phases meld into one another almost imperceptibly because of the piece-wise nature of city development. I call attention to the pioneering work of Marcial Echenique at Cambridge which was initially directed at evaluating planning proposals such as new roads or the location of industrial sites, but which in more recent years has found uses as an urban management system to estimate road pricing strategies, for example. At the Bartlett, Bill Hillier and his colleagues have contributed to micro-design of the urban environment through a consideration of the larger spatial syntax. Hillier has now been joined by Philip Steadman who has made a lifelong study of urban and building morphology, particularly in regard to energy uses. Mike Batty, an early pioneer in urban modelling and an established leader in GIS has established the independent Centre for Advanced Spatial Analysis.[6]

Design Machines

So much for the 'Ruskin' model – wouldn't dear John have hated it; I can see the stones of Venice turning over! Later, I reflected on the logic of this same process in the light of Charles Sanders Peirce's concepts. Recall, he had played an important role in the development of modern computational theory and practice. IBM owns the letter which diagrams his novel electrical circuits for the AND and OR operators. He did not accept the immutability of so-called natural laws, any more than Charles Babbage had done earlier using a computational argument; nor did he accept the sovereignty of the deductive method. His logic allowed three modes – deductive, inductive, and something he called abductive.

I used this classification to illustrate the cyclical logic of design in which collections of designs define types in terms of common features among designs; designs are defined by their type and the specific features which characterise them; and features are what designs of a certain type share. Peirce describes this trichotomy as

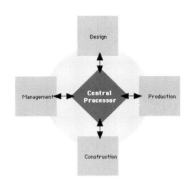

BOVE: A concurrent computer system for the uilding process presented at Ruskin College, xford, 1966
ELOW: A logical model of the design process. onel March, The Architecture of Form, Cambridge niversity Press, 1976

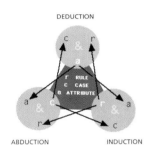

DEDUCTION

RULE
CASE
ATTRIBUTE

ABDUCTION   INDUCTION

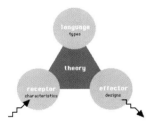

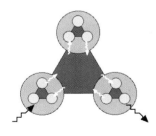

BOVE: Design Machine, George Stiny and Lionel March, 'Design Machines' in Planning and Design, 1981 ELOW: Design machines can be networked in series, parallel and in any combination

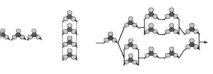

rule (my type), case (my design), and result (my feature). In my 1976 paper "The logic of design and the question of value," I proposed a computational model of the design process in these terms. I wrote, then, that abduction creates; deduction predicts; induction evaluates. At the risk of over-simplification: deduction is the *quod erat demonstrandum* mode of the mathematical and the theoretical sciences; induction the law seeking mode of the empirical sciences; and abduction is the novel, creative mode of the design process. Most human endeavours involve all three modes of reasoning to some degree, or other.

The next step in my consideration of the design process was taken with George Stiny in our paper 'Design Machines' based on his and James Gips' *Algorithmic Aesthetics*. This is a pragmatic device. It assumes that any intelligent system has both a receptor which recognizes events and things in the world, and an effector which allows the system to act upon the world in response. Something mediates in between. The conventional information–theoretic model had a processor which mediated between input and output – such was Herbert Simon's view. Our contribution is to see that there has to be some language which carries this mediation. If the leading intention of design is to give shape to some functioning object, then the primary language should be governed by a shape grammar. That is our argument.

On Multitudes and Magnitudes

In his celebrated English edition of Euclid's *Elements*, Sir Thomas Heath writes:

It is a remarkable fact that the theory of proportion is twice treated... in Book V with reference to magnitudes in general, and in Book VII with reference to the particular case of numbers.

Heath ponders why Euclid would wish to repeat his theorems, when the theorems for magnitudes include those for numbers – which meant rational numbers exclusively. He settles for 'tradition'. But I suggest that Euclid was acutely aware of the great computational divide between geometrical magnitudes and arithmetical multitudes: between shape and number. In my own historical researches, I have become aware of the beginnings of the modern passion for reducing numberless things to number. Among historians of mathematics, it is becoming increasingly appreciated that the artist, Piero della Francesca, was also 'the greatest mathematician of the fifteenth century'. His mathematical work may be characterized as the arithmetization of Euclid's geometry, that is, its digitization. Thus with the contribution of Piero della Francesca, together with Alberti's theory of perspective and his co-ordinate systems for map-making and three-dimensional description, the Italians had prepared the ground for the analytical geometry of Desargues and Descartes two centuries later. Le Corbusier liked to remind us, we all live in a Cartesian world. As you know, this world-view has been questioned. But the happy way that students play with geometry in AutoCAD – especially

the post-structuralist pretenders – tells me that very important lessons are being ignored: starting with the fact that particulate digits are the unreconcilable antagonists of shape (the very stuff of design).

GEOMETRY *IS NOT* **DIGITAL**

DIGITAL IS MULTITUDE
MULTITUDE IS **NUMBER**

GEOMETRY IS MAGNITUDE
MAGNITUDE IS **SHAPE**

The computational dilemma lies between

NUMBER *AND* **SHAPE**

Star Dust Fractal

Fractal geometry is nothing more than arithmetic in picture form masquerading as geometry in a multi-coloured pixal coat. Its obsessive emphasis on recursive similitude disturbs me profoundly. Undoubtedly this is because I have been in the shape grammar camp for the past 25 years, and we have known from the outset that fractals are an impoverished sub-set of shape grammars. I tried to convey this idea in a paper 'Rulebound Unruliness.'

I start with a typical fractal: the star dust. A simple shape rule carries two triangles in hour-glass formation to a hexagram – the star of David. Each hexagram has six scaled-down pairs of the original hour-glass formation. Recursive applications of the shape rule produce the star dust fractal. In passing, I note that the 'laws' of this universe can be determined, including one conservation law.

This is not all that might have happened in a shape computation. The hexagram has six hour-glass figures. If I choose one for rule application, I am left with just three. I may now choose another hour-glass figure in two distinct ways. One way corresponds to the choice made in the star dust fractal. The other, however, breaks the shape into one hour-glass figure and two distinct, non-touching triangles. Further, suppose the rule is to move a triangle 4/3 its length along one of its three axes, this produces the same result for the hour-glass, but releases the computation for more general applications under Euclidean transformations. The result of many recursive applications of this single rule looks quite unruly and contains 'degenerate' shapes other than triangles. The previous law of conservation no longer holds. In fact the possible universes are lawless in the usual scientific sense, but not without rule by design.

Miracles

Miraculous happenings, in Charles Babbage's understanding, may occur in a shape computation. Babbage employed a thought-experiment for his projected calculating engine in which he imagined the machine producing a sequence 'of natural numbers ... each succeeding its immediate antecedent by one'. Simply, 1, 2, 3, 4, 5, ... Induction would predict after many million repetitions of the rule n goes to $n + 1$, that this is the 'law,' or as Peirce would say, the 'habit,' of this

ABOVE AND RIGHT: The stardust fractal. The diagram shows the shape rule which takes an 'hour glass' into the 'star of David.' Recursive application of this rule in parallel leads, from top to bottom, to constellations of smaller and smaller stars
BELOW: A change of shape rule applied in sequence produces a random design which is not a fractal, and in which the generating triangles become corrupted (non-similarity). The previous 'natural' laws no longer apply. Yet the universe is rule governed. Based on Lionel March "Rulebound Unruliness," Planning and Design, 1996

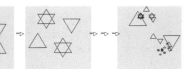

BELOW: A Turing-like machine in which a tape carries an image of a regular triangle moves over another regular triangle. The latter is always in the field of vision of the machine. The former comes into view and subsequently passes out of view. The machine reads only triangles and records the number it senses. Reading from left to right, top to bottom, are presented possible computational moments in the machine's operation. Based on Lionel March "Babbage's Miraculous Computation Revisited," Planning and Design, 1996

machine. But the programmer has pre-arranged for the rule to be broken and to introduce another. After an interminably long time, the 'law' changes again, and so on. Each change in habitual expectation appears as a miracle.

The problem about Babbage's example is that the rule changes. Imagine now the following Turing-like computation in a shape machine. A tape with a triangle inscribed on it is moved in equal steps over another triangle, opposed in orientation. The machine is only capable of recognizing complete triangles in its field of vision. The machine records the number of triangles seen. We know that there are two triangles. Bertrand Russell wrote in his *Introduction to Mathematical Philosophy*:

It must have required many ages to discover that a brace of pheasants and a couple of days were both instances of the number 2.

What if he had addressed the psychological problem that William James had set earlier in counting the number of triangles in the star of David – two large ones? six small ones? eight in all? or whatever? Substituting the phrase 'a pair of triangles' for a 'brace of pheasant,' or a 'couple of days,' would seriously confuse Russell's anthropological observation. You see, the logical atomist carefully chose his example to be 'atomic,' but shapes – other than points themselves – are not atomic.

The output sequence for the 'sum' of two triangles from our machine might read:

1...	for a long time while the moving triangle is out of view, then
2...	while the moving triangle is recognized as a triangle by the recordinghead, until
4...	the trailing edge of the moving triangle touches the forward apex of the fixed one, then
5...	while the moving triangle continues along its path, until
7...	the leading vertex of the moving triangle touches the back edge of the fixed triangle, then
8...	while the moving triangle continues along its path, until
6	the two trailing vertices of the moving triangle touch adjacent sides of the fixed, then
3...	while the moving triangle continues along its path, until
2...	the trailing edge of the moving triangle coincides with the trailing edge of the other, until
1...	the moving triangle moves out from the field of vision.

Shape arithmetic of this kind works in unexpected ways.

Set Structures on a Line

In my paper 'The smallest interesting world?', I adopted ideas which Ron Atkins had first brought to my attention, and which my colleagues Jeff Johnson and Yin-Seong Ho pursued at The Open University. The leading advocate of the approach today is Rudolf Wille of the Technical University Darmstadt. I recommend his book, *Formal Concept Analysis*, with Bernard Ganter. It raises many fundamental issues. I quote from the 'radical conventionalism' of the Polish philosopher, Adjudkiewicz:

No articulated judgement is absolutely forced on us by the data of experience. Experiential data do indeed force us to accept certain judgements if also we are based in a particular conceptual apparatus. However, if we change this conceptual apparatus, we are freed of the necessity of accepting these judgements despite the presence of the same experiential data.

The conceptual apparatus is the Galois lattice. This

requires the world to be seen as objects and features, an engineering view that is essentially Cartesian. The smallest interesting world is, I propose, a line and its two defining endpoints. The point alone is a point alone, and that is its sum interest: the ultimate 'Being.' You cannot say that about a line which is all 'becoming,' it can become anything we want it to be. For illustrative purposes imagine a GRAY rod with distinguishable spheres at each end to represent the endpoints, say, BLACK and WHITE. We look at the parts of such a rod. According to the set-theoretic concepts we have adopted as convention, these are eight in number, marked by colours.

Structures depicted as Lattices

Different logical structures may be constructed depending on how we look at the rod. If all the parts can be recognized separately, all eight must be taken into account:

1. BLACK–GRAY–WHITE
2. BLACK–GRAY
3. BLACK——WHITE
4. GRAY–WHITE
5. BLACK
6. GRAY
7. WHITE
8. [empty part]

The logical object/feature structure of this is Boolean.

Under symmetry, the endpoints would be indistinguish-able, say, both are BLACK (a condition of colour-blindness):

1. BLACK–GRAY–BLACK
2. BLACK–GRAY
3. BLACK——BLACK
4. BLACK
5. GRAY
6. [empty part]

The logical structure is 'intuitionist,' or Brouwerian. The Blakean 'Divinity of Yes and No' is put to rest. The excluded middle does not hold. If there is said to be an 'A' there is only the possibility of a 'pseudo not-A.' It may be possible for A and not-A to logically coexist, but we shall never be certain.

But if an isolated point is rejected as not being a part of the line, since a line cannot be defined by one point alone, then there are just five parts (accepting the empty part for tidiness):

1. BLACK–GRAY–BLACK
2. BLACK–GRAY
3. BLACK——BLACK
4. GRAY
5. [empty part]

This structure is 'quantum,' since it exhibits the five point lattice identified in 1936 by von Neumann and Birkhoff as characteristic of the logic of quantum mechanics. Intuitionistic and quantum logics are usually identified with problems of infinite sequences in mathematical induction and with subatomic physics, but here they are at the end of designer's pencil whenever a line is struck between two endpoints.

A Line as Shape

This previous example is set grammatical, or, as Stiny is prone to remark, 'tinker-toy' ready-made bits and

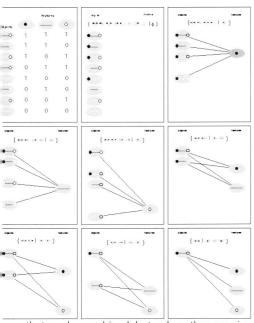

ABOVE: A conventional line and its discrete parts
LEFT: The relationship between objects (sub-assemblies) and features (basic elements, points and line). Top left, zero-matrix of relationships. The remaining eight boxes show maximal cliques for objects/features. Based on Lionel March "The Smallest Interesting World," Planning and Design, 1996
BELOW: Boolean lattice of objects/features for the conventional line derived from the Galois connection
RIGHT: Galois lattices of line in which: top: the endpoints are distinguishable (Boolean); middle: the endpoints are indistinguishable (Brouwerian, intuitionistic); bottom: a single endpoint, standing alone, is discounted (quantum)

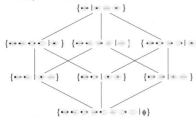

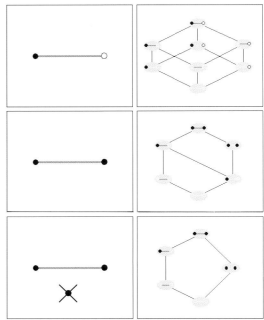

eces that can be combined, but only as they are given. ven so, it demonstrates within these limitations that a ne has no single definitive structure. In fact, Stiny has id that "lines can be subdivided into segments in any

ay whatsoever," and that such segments are "lines of on-zero length." As Chris Earl pointed out to me, this llies with Blake's loathing of Newtonian 'atoms':

a Line is a Line in its Minutest Subdivisions: Strait or rooked It is Itself & Not Intermeasureable with or by ny Thing Else.

A line is not a set of points. Its boundary is defined y the two endpoints, but everything else is line. There e no units, or 'atoms', that constitute the line. The very ention of unit takes us back to numbers, and shapes e not numbers. Of course, among our choices is to sub- vide a line in units – an arbitrary choice. Or to subdivide in discrete segments that touch, but do not overlap – an bitrary choice again. Or they overlap in multiple ways.

rrival

have journeyed from simplistic global calculations, rough land use and built form studies, to the design rocess, and on to some reflections on digital and ape computations. I have challenged some assump- ons of conventional wisdom arising from studies of esign and designs over the past forty years – especially ose related to computation. My recent interest in edieval and renaissance practices has much to do ith trying to appreciate why we have tendencies to ink in the ways that we do as a matter of habit. The storian, Alfred W Crosby, has written perceptively on is in *The Measure of Reality: Quantification and /estern Society, 1250-1600*. Margaret Wertheim *thagoras' Trousers: God, Physics, and the Gender /ars* makes for salutary and complementary reading. As an early advocate of the 'quantitative revolution' the spatial sciences, I have no regrets. Much has been chieved. But the success should not blind us to faults in ne foundations. The creative process, the generation of

designs, is still very much on the back-burner where Herbert Simon placed it in *The Sciences of the Artificial*, or Myron Tribus in *Rational Descriptions, Decisions and Designs*. Theirs was an engineer's vision of design where there are primitive elements, hierarchical organization of components and sub-assemblies, and finding satisfactory values of parameters in a schemata is the prime task.

Creating the schemata in the first place is surely the key issue for creative designing. Chance techniques promoted in school studios largely succeed with the untutored stud- ent since apparent novelty is produced. But as I have said in my conclusion to "The Smallest Interesting World?":

The intuitive, even instinctual, sense, which designers have, that rational thought must be transcended in the creative process, may derive from their limited perspec- tive on rationality. The crude contrast often drawn between science and art is delineated more by narrowly supposing that science works to a single logic and a singular method, than by sweepingly claiming that design is beyond logic and subject only to gut feeling. What is required is an appreciation of a licentious rationality in both art and science.

And then:

Contrary to conventional wisdom, rationality does not flourish in the presence of objective certainty, but actually thrives around subjective volition. To be rational requires the willingness to restructure the world on each contin- gent occasion, or in just two words, TO DESIGN.

George Stiny shows that Turing computations may be conducted on shapes in place of numbers, and provides a concrete example to satisfy Hobbes' conjecture about the act of non-numerical 'ratiocination.' As thought, a shape computation is not digital, yet for its execution, digital methods of some kind must be employed. Even if one imagines some analogue computer that operates on shapes directly, there will still be matters of resol- ution even at the quantum level. Geometry is pure thought, it does not exist in the corporeal world. Yet,

surely, in their minds the best designers manipulate shapes with considerable geometrical agility, knowing that magnitudes can always be fudged to fit the numerical expediency of concrete production.

A criticism of shape grammarians is that they rarely compute on computers. Many of their examples are hands on, paper and pencil computations. The reason is clear. Too immediate a reliance on the computer necessarily encourages thinking about shapes digitally. Yet thinking about shapes requires more syntactic flexibility, more semantic ambiguity, more pragmatic continuity than any analogy with number and arithmetic permits or current digital technology can provide. Especially, most if not all digital systems predefine, preclassify, and prestructure the worlds they represent. From the small examples I have given today, and the work of my close colleagues over the past forty years, I hope you will see that creative design requires open lines of thought in which the world is not reduced to digits.

How House, Silver Lake, Los Angeles
6 December 1999

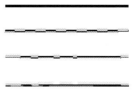

NOTES
1. *I live in the United States where I do not have to suffer the homogenization and globalization of the metric system — not yet anyway.*
2. *Yes, echoes of Louis Kahn's 'service-served' dichotomy.*
3. *See* Urban Space and Structures, *1972*
4. *These would have to be taken from Froebel's* Sixth Gift
5. *While working with Ed Hoskins at Applied Research of Cambridge*
6. *In tandem with the Bartlett, at University College London.*

Wolf Prix

In Between
OR Only Unstable Points can be Points of Departure

*"Be realistic.
Think the impossible"*
Ernesto Che Guevara

OPPOSITE: The Tower of Babel. Detail
RIGHT: Ernesto Che Guevara,
Republic of Argentina, postage
stamps, commemorative issue
fortuitously coinciding with the
Buenos Aires Bienal

The other day I read a book about architecture which divided the architecture of today into two schools: the hi-tech school; and "building boxes." But I would call the hi-tech guys "nineteenth- century engineers," and the box builders the "prophets of obedience."

But it is too simple to divide architecture into two schools. There must be a third way of thinking. And to describe this third way, I would like to quote one of your countrymen: Che Guevara. He said – and this is very important – "Be realistic. Think the impossible."

The book I read said that so-called deconstructivist architecture is over, because dynamic shapes and forms have gone out of fashion. I think the author confused many things: first of all, he is confused about what is dynamic. Then he has confused deconstructivist architecture with architecture *in toto*. I think there is a misunderstanding that must be clarified because they call us deconstructivists and blame us for crazy forms, but the deconstructivist method of thinking is related to Jacques Derrida's method of analytic thinking and analysing text in order to question the rational way of thinking in Europe. That is deconstructivist architecture – an architecture that questions the rationality of our life in Europe today.

I should like to define some paradigms at the forefront of our work in the last couple of years. If you asked me how I would define architecture I would say that architecture does not complete function but is rather the improvement of the illusion of reality. The eye is the most powerful organ to perceive architecture but it is not the only organ. To experience space you have to use your body as well. It means that you can read the cross section or the plan but in order to experience it you have to walk through it. The eye, and mistrusting the eye, the brain. There is research from MIT which suggests that, unlike analogue images, digitised images do not enter the long-term memory but only the short term memory and I think this will be revolutionary in the next few years. You have to imagine that if you draw only on the computer and if you see movies only in digitised form, you can go to the same movie two weeks later and you will see it as a new work.

A German writer has defined upcoming society by comparing a nomad with contemporary man. He says that a guy who at the airport finds at the right time the right plane to take him to the right place, compared to a nomad who finds the tracks through the desert by the stars is a non-complex-thinking, one-dimensional guy. What does this mean? I think we are going towards a more and more complex society, which means that for architecture complex solutions do not have simple answers. Six thousand years ago mankind decided which way he had to go, namely, the change from a matriarchal system into patriarchal societies. And you can read that in city plans.

When people describe our architecture they always say it is disquieting and chaotic. So what is the opposite of disquieting and chaotic? It is, of course, law and order.

A polemic against simplifying architecture too much is that a chicken has to learn two images in order to survive feeding in a meadow: it can stay if it sees a goose but it has to run if it sees a falcon. The astonishing thing is that the chicken does not have to see the complex movement of the bird. It runs if it sees one abstraction and it stays if it sees another abstraction. This means that if you reduce your thinking too much there is a danger that you will share the point of view of a chicken.

But what can we say about the future of architecture? There are a lot of theories about how architecture should be explained in the future. We have another theory, one more theory. What we want to do is to finish the Tower of Babel. The Tower of Babel was prevented from being completed by an authority that brought the confusion of language to our society. We think that we have to confuse our language again in order to acquire the variety and complexity needed to complete the Tower of Babel.

Actually the title of this lecture should be that only unstable points can be points of departure. And looking for unstable points and points of departure that describe the network of a rigid system has been at the forefront of our work for perhaps the past ten or fifteen years. And we try to find it by looking at the ground plan in the same way that we look at the cross section, which means that the cross section and the ground plan are equal to each other and in between there is space which is, of course, liquid. We try to define the point of departure by finding the unstable points and trying to define the liquid spaces as well. We did this step by step in our winning entry for Moulins Sénart and it led to a master plan but the most interesting thing is that we defined the unstable points by supporting the weaker parts. In this case the low density structures were stronger than the high density structures meaning that in a short time these points were very valuable on many levels. Actually, it became not a two-dimensional but a three-dimensional master plan although it is not, of course, a proposal for buildings.

A guy who at the airport finds at the right time the right plane to take him to the right place, compared to a nomad who finds the tracks through the desert by the stars is a non-complex-thinking, one-dimensional guy.

And there is another code in the Moulins Sénart project. The code of getting back public spaces. In Europe we are in danger of losing public spaces because the cities are broke: they have to sell the ground and the land to investors, and developers are doing what they have to do: they have to squeeze money out of every square metre, which means that they create only monofunctional, capitalistic structures. We architects have to gain public space by inventing strategies and one of these strategies is that we propose in this case that every 50m there must be an area for free public use.

It was fifteen years ago now that we were able to realise one of these ideas, namely the idea of public space in the middle of a building. In a social housing project in Vienna, an eighteen metre high-rise, mid-rise, and in between these two zones where the normal building goes into the high rise codes and rules there is a free zone which people can use as they wish. There are other issues as well. The slanted shapes of the leaning towers define the urban space in a very specific way and the facades support the climate. The typology of the high rise is inverted so that each floor is different. Free space in the middle of a high rise is open to every inhabitant and it is, of course, the idea of a vertical city.

For the cinema complex in Dresden we had to define an urban area and we did it by exchanging the axial thinking by tensions and vectors and thus made room in an area connected to an existing cinema for the new cinema which was to house auditoriums with 3000 seats. By studying the dynamic of the city plan and the dynamic of the people flow and overlaying it, a certain kind of model came out which is not only defined by concrete, but also by light, in a reference to the movies. Light as a building material can only be used when it's dark. So if you look at cities in the daytime and at night-time, they are very, very different. And so these are the two levels we played on. The space sequences are reduced to a building, a building which consists of two parts: the block where the cinemas are organised and the lobby. Usually, the lobby is only the box office where you can buy tickets. But here we made an urban balcony out of this simple lobby in order to get the point of departure for the development in the city of Dresden. If you look at the city plan the new cinema is at a strategic point. It's close to the old part of the city; it's new because it was terribly bombed in the Second World War and rebuilt in the idea of a misunderstood modernist architecture. There are a lot of slabs and actually the new ideas for city planning are not so far from what exists here. We connected the cinema block visually to the existing cinema and we made the cinema a point of departure on the one hand and the possibility for a passage on the other hand. This means that this building is a transitorial building. You can walk through it to go to the cinemas but you can also cross through it. The area is low density now but, because of the cinema, there will be an increasing density.

The other thing was the typology. The typology of the cinema complex reads like that in every city. The auditoriums are stabled one above the other and in front there is a kind of glass lobby. What we did in order to get more freedom and in order to provide the passage from one street to the other was to introduce the concept of cantilevering. This shows the typology of the building, the concrete slab where the auditoriums are packed and in front there is - not a soft volume - it's more than just a volume, it's like a theatre, an introduction to the movies on the one hand and the passage on the other hand. If you go to your client and say I want to build a building that is cantilevered, normally he will fire you because everyone knows that cantilevering is much more expensive than building a straightforward block, a box. But we could prove in this case that if the client would cantilever the whole building in order to get a passage through the building he would have to buy less land than if it were a block as he would only have to pay for the air rights of the building and so the expenses of the cantilevering were equal to the expenses of buying the land.

There was another issue. How could we use this crystal-like building for more than just box offices. How could we manoeuvre within the volume to show that the time of central perspective is over. I believe that central perspectives are obsolete now that man has conquered outer space where there is no gravity and people can roll around their own body.

Introducing sculptures in space on the one hand defines the space and on the other are a kind of built video clip. People walking through experience a very different image from each point of view.

Studying how this could work led back to a project we did three years ago, a project for a kind of museum of knowledge in Kyoto where we carved out a volume which is the reading area and placed the shape right in front of the building like a sculpture in space defining the space at one end and informing people that something is happening in the block.

The other issue, as you will see later, is dissolving the facade from the building. In a research building in Austria we glazed the facade that controls the light and therefore the climate in the building. We placed it right in front of the building and we dissolved it from the building so that we created an in-between space that has no function and that people can use as they wish.

Back to the sculptures in space at the cinema in Dresden. They are a kind of enlargement of the concrete block because the columns are concrete. On the other hand, using metal in this way increases the crystal which is constructed of metal and glass. So there are two movements in this space showing that there is a transition action.

The sculptures in space move out from the concrete block; the pillars are concrete and the others are metal moving into the concrete blocks. There are two movements. Then we use the kind of light concept that is different in summer and in winter and in the daytime and the evening because it changes from warm light from the floor to cold light from the top and there are different shades according to the time of year as well. When people asked us years ago what our role models in architecture were , we always answered the Rolling Stones, especially Richard playing guitar solo in *Gimme Shelter.* It is exactly the same tension that we want to give. It was kind of true.

The finished cinema looks different from every side. We call it the Janus-headed concept. At least two points of views, two views. If you walk around you can read it from every side and it is very different. The facade we placed on the concrete, on one side it's a metal gridded facade and it is fascinating because when the light is right and the sun is shining and hitting this facade sometimes it looks like liquid glass. And this is what we would call liquid space: it defines the urban space but it doesn't close it. Liquid architecture. It is exactly 40m high and you have to walk up in order to go to the cinemas and there are a lot of stairs and a lot of ramps and bridges. One bridge leads nowhere – we call it the bridge of the architects; it is the bridge of the architects because we were standing up there looking down when the building was opened.

We think that we have to confuse our language again in order to acquire the variety and complexity needed to complete the Tower of Babel.

The cinemas are placed 12m and 16m high and there is no escalator because we saved the money in order to make the lobby bigger. Of course there is an elevator for the disabled. People use this as a built video clip, stomping around and playing at being actors, using the stairs for performances.

The cinema changes dramatically when it's getting dark so it's really two buildings, one in daylight, another one at night. The crystal is not a glowing crystal, and it is not the perfect way to describe it because a crystal is symmetrical and this is not a symmetrical building but what we are doing is investigating liquid space in an urban project.

There are two stories I would like to tell you before I close. The first is that Rem tells us that architects are always hostages who say "We are fine" when they are asked how they are doing with a pistol to their head. I like this story very much but I like the story of Cimino which he tells in his movie *The Deer Hunter* much better. It is a story about the Viet Cong and the Vietnam war. Two friends, Robert de Niro and Christopher Walken are caught by the Viet Cong and they have to play Russian roulette. Robert de Niro starts, everything went well and he says "Give me a second bullet." His friend almost has a nervous breakdown and says "Try it. Do it." And he did it and it went well again. So he asked for a third bullet. When he got the third bullet he shot through the three guards and they escaped. So I think we have to triple the risk in order to make architecture. I started with a quote from your countryman Che Guevara and I would like to conclude with a quote from him: "Venceremos!"

Article based on lectures given at the BA Bienal.

Ignasí de Solà Morales

Present and Futures

"Now is tomorrow," says a line from a poem by the Catalan poet Miquel Martí í Pol. Architectural culture has for too long been living in nostalgia. Architects speak of architecture of the past: of the recent past or of a thousand years ago. The progressive transformation of culture into a museum piece has led to a view dominated by the values of what history has established as a heritage that weighs upon the present.

The crisis of modernity has generated a blockage to viewing the future with anything but a blinding admiration for the great landmarks of architectural history.

The peripheries of all the big cities have grown spectacularly in the last thirty years as fruit of an urban revolution the significance of which has no precedent in the history of humanity.

The situation we have reached is one of genuine schizophrenia in architectural culture: on the one hand, nostalgia for the past; on the other, the uneasy conscience of the present.

Furthermore, there is no discourse to explain and assume the magnitude of what is actually happening.

What is needed, immediately, is a new "Rappel à Messieurs les architectes" like Le Corbusier's famous call to order in "Vers une architecture."

To eyes that do not see there is no point in showing what the engineers are doing, as they

did in the twenties, but what we ourselves are doing, what architecture is doing to respond to the imperious demands of new needs and extensions, new colonisations, new technologies.

When in London, New York, Istanbul or Barcelona we close our eyes to most of their buildings, while guide books show us exquisite objects, old buildings and districts, as if these were the true essence of these cities and their architecture.

We spend most of our life in office and business centres, on sports fields, at airports and metro stations, in peripheral homes and shopping centres. However, such architecture seems banal, often sad; it lacks the quality we believe we find in the city and in traditional architecture.

In fact, though, things could seem not to be thus. We have not yet learned to dominate movement, telematization, provisional qualities and extension. We have no clear replies to the phenomena of building in constant change, accu-mulation, the disassociation between the need to create a rhetorical place and to contribute to public spaces where interaction does not become unbearable.

These are the problems we should examine, not only from the viewpoint of city planning but also, and more especially, from that of constructing architecture.

Paper contributed to the Hydra Symposium in honour of Dimitri Fatouros

'Three directions in architecture' is accompanied by paintings and designs by the author.
ABOVE: Albero argentino per Alexandra (Argentinian tree for Alexandra)
OPPOSITE: Movimento casuale (Casual movement)

Franco Purini

Three Directions for Architecture

In the rich countries that occupy a key position in the globalisation of the economy, architecture no longer plays an active role. Its duty to provide solutions to basic needs has now been exhausted since the age of modern architecture has achieved the results it had been pursuing for two centuries.

This is a decisive turning point in the history of architecture because the fact that it has achieved all its objectives does not signify its end. Architecture is the physical expression of human reflection on habitat. That is why we cannot speak of the "death" of architecture. If we translate freely one of Karl Marx's concepts and apply it to architecture, we can say that "the art of building" has passed from the structural to the super-structural. Post-modernism, which is not the same thing as the "post-modern state," is the realisation of this situation, never previously experienced, and deconstruction its most radical expression. This is a situation of the "superfluous." Today the state of architecture is substantially superfluous. At least insofar as it is possible to pursue this state, it appears to be stable and destined to spread.

Therefore, architecture is no longer what it was until a few years ago, that is the art or the discipline for resolving such concrete and urgent problems as the "housing question," to quote Engels, or the complex growth of the city and its public places. Today, architecture is no longer authentically itself but merely a representation of itself. It constitutes the notes to a text that has already been written. This transition from reality to representation has an important echo in another transformation that architecture has undergone in today's media culture: the separation of the building from its image. The building as "physical object" has lost much of its meaning: what counts now is its simulacrum projected onto the international information circuit, giving rise to the new concept of the "architectural body," a concept synthesised in the oxymoron "immaterial body," which summarises the schizophrenic nature of something – the building – divided into two irreconcilable realities. The media culture survives despite the entropy of communication; communication that is

trying to become ever more instantaneous, precise and direct, and at the same time more extensive. In juxtaposition with a process of continuous, unstoppable "degradation," the message comes across with more and more emphasis, full of superimposed signals, ever more casual and concise. This situation certainly does not call for a rejection of the "apocalyptic" *mass media* of Umberto Eco nor for naive, enthusiastic endorsements. Perhaps the architect has to be convinced of the need for a different form of communication, one that is meant to be both difficult and broken up, sown like a labyrinth of dead ends. This is not a dubious, elitist demand for hermeticism; it is because something that requires no effort has no importance. A message that is easily received is immediately forgotten. To counteract the entropy of communication and the confusion created by the media there is a need for a selective transmission of signals to provide a "route for the initiated" through "dialectic buildings," capable of posing questions and giving answers. Even though this position is somewhat elitist, the present degeneration of information – one of the worst results of globalisation – means that there are no credible alternatives.

Today, architecture is no longer authentically itself but merely a representation of itself

And so how does architecture react when confronted with the fact that it has suddenly become "superfluous?" It appears to have chosen three ways of finding a new role, which will be presented in order of their complexity.

The first one can be defined as the "exaggeration of the functions of a building or group of buildings" with the double objective of giving back to architecture the lost ability to resolve primary problems, while at the same time conferring once more on the architect great contractual power. Here, architecture overvalues its own technical qualities – *firmitas* and *utilitas* in Vitruvius's words – for recovering the centrality of a role now in decline. This general attitude can be seen in three design tendencies: hi-tech; the sense of responsibility for the building from the point of view of a socio/psycho/existential complexity; and the utopia of "environmental control."

The first tendency favours technological innovation and makes it spectacular by treating the building as an -system. Materials are treated in such a way as to no longer bear traces of their "earthly" origin but to allude to their "synthetic" nature. The clear and the transparent predominate; structures are complicated for no real functional reason; recourse to prefabrication, now approaching cult status, leads to the use of technologies such as those of aeronautics and space science which are unnecessary in architecture. But flight does not only apply to an evocation of sophisticated aeronautical technologies. Common references to the wing form, to the hollow bone structure of birds or the cartilage of insects inspire the design of many projects, as do waves, vibrations, and dynamic air flows. And so flight becomes a metaphor for a superior, immaterial, spiritual journey. But it is a flight which, even more than traditional construction, reveals the static destiny of architecture, which must always remain rooted in the ground.

The commitment to the project displayed in hi-tech is obvious. Each detail is emphasised and dramatised. Details are hyperrealist, mannerist, and essentially decorative. There is no "respite" for the user or the observer; each part of the building is charged with a rhetorical anxiety expressed by a substantial amount of "overdesign." As for the materials, a value is conferred on them that transcends technique and touches on a symbolic or even mystical/esoteric content, almost as if the architect is a new alchemist capable of releasing, through his contact with the elements, the cosmic energy imprisoned in the crystals, special metals, and resins so they lose their original character.

The preference of many architects for hi-tech may derive from the fact that it is impossible in contemporary culture to agree on a common idea of "*venustas*," and so in order to demonstrate that his work is innovative, the project-maker is reduced to concentrating his efforts on the functional and technical aspects of construction, the only ones on which it is relatively easy to agree. This is also one of the consequences of the "age of technology" of which Heidegger speaks.

The second tendency is related to the first and comprises the attribution of a determinant role to the building with respect to the socio/psycho/existential values of the users of the architectural spaces. Their conformity, the spaces that compose them, the light that pervades them, assume – within this perspective – a "formative" role; one that does not tolerate any errors that would lead to a bad quality of life for the inhabitants or irreparable breakdowns in their environment and in their private and social life. The great Dutch architect Aldo van Eyck is undoubtedly the best known leader of this tendency, which also comprises the work of such architects as Giancarlo de Carlo. Going beyond the legal aspect, the importance of architecture for the balance of both the individual and society gives rise to complicated rituals of "participation." This is a practice where the architects abandon the major aspect of their responsibilities – the one relating to "form" – but in return the users do nothing but project demands for mass culture stereotypes.

The third tendency represents an extension and radicalisation of hi-tech. With ecological problems in all their magnitude and urgency as his starting point, the architect claims the necessity of controlling the environment, a control that is translated into standard procedures, in which an idealistic and abstract "utopism" takes on a strong, disconcerting alliance with a positivist confidence in its scientific potential. The complexity of the architectural phenomenon, its formal and semantic nature are resolved within a planned and processed functionality. The passwords "transformability," "adaptability," and "intelligence," outline a "politically correct" role for the building, which is most often revealed to be a propaganda and technological illusion. Behind this design tendency is the consistent ideological component of an integrating matrix, which by way of an absolution that is both ingenuous and approximates the rationalised capacities of the design concept, claims to give new meaning to the idea of nature itself. All of this leads to the teaching of a fundamental, prophetic "ecological ethic" to save the planet from future destruction. The result is a paradox. The building must not "pollute" the environment and it therefore interacts with the outside only in a "neutralised," "hygienic" manner; at the same time it constitutes a "shelter" from the same environment, which subliminally remains threatening. In this way, the air is "corrected" by air-conditioners, filters, and obligatory replacement; the light is altered, and even rationed, as though it were harmful; the use and duration demands placed on materials are counterproductive in relation to the building itself. This line starts with the Crystal Palace, passes through Buckminster Fuller's "enlightened" dream of pacific militarisation (of the planet) and the successive futuristic projections of Archigram, until it finally arrives at the "creative delirium" of a Foster coming up against an insuperable "poetic" limit. A hi-tech work seeks to express the future and therefore wants to remain forever young, intact, ablaze in its unspoilt glory: but unfortunately it ages, and gradually rust finds its way under the coatings, the glazing darkens, the joints become loose. The eternal promise of youth, the promise of eternal youth prove to be not merely an illusion but totally wrong. And so because of a rather arrogant decision, time reacquires all its rights.

The second answer to the transformation of architecture into a "superfluous" activity is to be found in its direct relationship with art. In this case too, there are three design tendencies. The first one was born years ago at the Cooper Union in New York and the Architectural Association in London. It can be expressed by the slogan "architecture is like the other arts," meaning that architecture, by becoming "superfluous," has acquired the same "inutility" as art – which has no purpose other than itself, and so refers only to itself. And so the architect becomes a sculptor, like Gehry or Eisenman. Gehry has abandoned his deconstructivist period for an expressionism of "deformation" where Moebius geometries are combined with baroque accents imbued with

a special biomorphism. In his latest buildings he appears to suggest a deep, solitary meditation on the decline of the body of a living being – either human or an imaginary animal – considered as an "analogous body" of the architecture of the last century. His interiors tragically hint at the intimate cavities of an organism, exposed by cruel but necessary dissection. As in Leonardo's anatomical designs, his plans and sections reveal – like the remains of some gory investigation – the end of an era going back to the spectacular visions of a Finsterlin or a Kiesler. Eisenman recites the same theme, but by exploring a totally "mineralised" world, a world of "artificial syntheses" that speaks of silicon chips and quartz, and revels in the broken line as an emblem of acute aggressiveness. But these experiences – and others related to them – each in their own way pose an insoluble problem. As sculptures (large urban sculptures, to which function is only afterwards attributed – even if it is done with great care) such works reduce the "use" to mere filling. Viewed as architecture, they degrade sculpture to a tool. In other words, the identification of archi-tecture with sculpture cannot constitute a valid direction for research because it inevitably leads to the removal of "meaning" from both art forms, a loss that from a heroically Promethean perspective is both noble and to a certain extent necessary.

The second design tendency consists of "adapting" artistic research for architecture, by popularising, diverting and then neutralising them. Art is conceived as a repertoire of stylistic names: it is plastic or conceptual, minimalist or arte povere, neo-expressionist or pop, that are reduced to mere "ornaments," formal adjectives, prestigious in tone, that should confer on the project a more solid and obvious cultural gloss. This is a very prevalent attitude among "professional" architects who are resentful – at times hysterically so – of the changes in formal styles that today occur at an ever more accelerated pace. In this way, a futuristic dream materialises of an architecture that dissolves into the illuminations of an urban setting as a sign of the regenerative "desecration" of its own authenticity, as in many buildings by Nouvel; as decoration, as a consumer "gadget," in the same way that the difficult and deeply thought out experiences of many minimalists – experiences that are totally ontological and aristocratically autonomous – nourish, with an inevitable loss of semantic density, much of Herzog and de Meuron's work. On a lower level they proliferate in Jean Arp's treatment of curves, the combinations of materials in the work of Beuys or Kounellis, the imitations of nature by Long and Serra.

The third tendency of this group appears the most reliable, although undoubtedly less striking by comparison. The archi-tect does not create sculptures, nor introduce elements of pure art into his work (although they are present). He points out that art is the only form of human expression that can define itself, by pronouncing as art what was not art before. Reflecting from this perspective, which goes beyond absolute freedom, the architect is restricted to believing that archi-tecture – a very particular art – has some possibility of self-definition. This is an element capable of contrasting what is a necessary conventional – and thus "inactive" – component of architecture with a component expressed in the typology. A fundamental category that will be seen as the "invariable structure" of the project and at the same time as the entity in the creative act that transcends itself, according to Argan.

The third and final answer to the discovery that architecture has become "superfluous" and one that appears at the outset to be the most promising, is the strategy of "renaming" the existing. What exists is no longer, as Le Corbusier believed at the time of the *Plan Voisin*, an obstacle to transformation, but the condition that makes trans-formation possible. Architecture faces up to reality and gives all its components a new name bestowing on them a new identity and a new coherence. It did this in 1989, after the tragedy of ex-Yugoslavia, after the great emigration from Eastern Europe, Africa, and Asia towards the wealthy West. At Kuala Lumpur, it proudly raises Pelli's twin towers – one of the most exciting "gateways" to the new millennium – while Sumatra burns its forests wiping out the towering metal spires of the Argentinean architect in a cloud of scorching fog. The "brave century" has delivered to humanity a world where the minority who waste immense resources – think of hi-tech and its mental and material energy costs – confront the majority who struggle in conditions of endemic misery. Half of the inhabitants of the planet have never made a phone call at a time when satellites are weaving ever more perfect and pervasive communication nets. Within this context of the "end of the story" architecture has the duty to accept, as part of being superfluous, the humble task of "describing" habitat to put it on the proper footing to acquire a new self-consciousness.

The eternal promise of youth, or the promise of eternal youth, prove to be not merely an illusion but totally wrong

In this direction, research can also distinguish three alternatives. The first is an "historical renaming." It consists of a narrative formality of "vertical" type that confronts the determinant question of a renewed nomenclature of the existing and its internal hierarchies. It is the "renaming" of Tafuri, which creates values and dis-values under the spectrum of a judgement that is both ethical and aesthetic, where the bottom line is the ultimate renunciation, the premeditated absence of the senses. Opposed to that "vertical" model is the "renaming of the present," a "horizontal" renaming that functions with no hierarchies, accepting with the "pity" of the layman all that falls under the observer's eye in its own neutral state. Things are observed through a "Wenders" eye that searches for the internal structure outside the ideology itself – assuming that this is possible. The "values" of historical renaming are replaced by the "connections" between objects, phenomena, events. Rogers, Muratori, Samonà, the initiators of this tendency, introduced at the end of the 1950s the importance of "environmental pre-existence" as an "active" presence rather than mere historical documents. This inter-pretation continued in Gregotti's hypothesis of "modification," set out in his journal "Casabella." This pro-posal foresees an essential role for the image of the existent, an existent "polarised" by the determinism of the project, and

Studio sulla città probabile (Study for the probable city)

therefore totally re-created by the poetic imagination. The third form of the commitment to give a new statute to the existent, whose image is worn out, is the "renaming of the future." It consists of a "project for the re-foundation" of the existent that does not regard it as things that simply "are," the population of physical entities that lie in the world "mechanically." What exists – *to exist* from the Latin *ex-sistere*, "coming from" – is the fruit of a conscious action to "construct" a reality. From that point of view, the existent is also what could be and is not, what could have been but was not, what has been and is no longer (as Freud wrote regarding Rome), what could not be and is not, what could not be and is. In this way time curves and touches on casual points, against which a change of seasons and things occurs; everything flows in a "discontinuous continuity." The fragment is not intended

in an esthetical sense nor considered as a renunciation of an opposition of an inaccessible or non-actual totality but as the product of an "analytical incident" it has the capacity to ignite in a spatial and material instant the flash of language. An architectural word, alight and interrupted, intercepted through the *"reverie"* of which Gaston Bachelard wrote many years ago. This inflation of the chrono-topical can be translated into figurative flashes that disclose unexplored territories of imagery, more adventurous than the pure fascinating and infinite "neo-neural" networks of cyberspace. A sense of imminent danger is configured as the basis of each aesthetic experience that "re-creates" the existent from the existent as if by an improvised magic descending on the world.

The architectural project that is born from having "renamed the existent in the future" is constructed in three

Il muro rosso (The red wall)

phases. The first is the act of "recognising," which is an act of belonging; the second is an act of "appropriation" of something essentially sympathetic to the other or to those things that are outside the subject or which the subject can "dismiss" as external to itself; the third is the act of "difference," a movement, an improvised deviation that adds meaning to an object, an added value of an eminently esthetic nature that reinforces the knowledge that the subject – the architect – has his defined place in the world. In this way identity is no longer defined as an autonomous entity but as a variable relationship beyond that which is to be built, that is also, even for a brief period, common ground. This establishment of a meeting point is one of the primary objectives of every "naming."

It was stated at the beginning that architecture which has revealed itself to be "superfluous today" and is anxiously searching for a new role that will illuminate the way forward, is the final goal. The first method for counteracting the special effects that hi-tech borrows from the cinema, psychological exasperation, and the cosmic delirium of total control of the environment, is to rediscover architecture's primary role; the second method is to counteract the output of nervously neo-expressionist artist/architects, leaving open the third way, a way that is born out of the profound and motivated choice of the superfluous as a means to apparently marginal, hermetic work that is the simple narration of the possible roles of the physical world through the patient enumeration of the objects, buildings and the signs that compose it. Objects, buildings, and signs like people, people who know that identity is a matter of recognition of the other and the elsewhere.

Itsuko Hasegawa

Floating Public Space

On the design of the Niigata Performing Arts Centre

Island Hopping

The Niigata Performing Arts Centre is an extremely complex project and the search for a simple metaphor to summarise its fundamental concept was a long one. Recently I have been using the term 'island hopping' for this purpose, with its implied imagery of light and loose, non-linear movement. As opposed to more closed systems, 'island hopping' implies a choice of paths, connections, and disconnections – a freedom that I am striving to incorporate into my architecture. Translated into landscape, it might be interpreted in the guise of floating green islands, or archipelagos, another metaphor I shall return to later.

Over the past ten years, consideration of the waterfront transition zone between port and city has been an important part of my work. A study of these complex edges, with their plurality of life, unique rhythms, and involved interrelationships, has given rise to an understanding of how these properties might relate to architecture itself. This research has led to the concept of 'island hopping' where the process of making architecture is likened to an archipelago, an eccentric island pattern. It is a poetic act, similar in spirit to the composition and performance of music.

In the case of the Yamanashi Fruit Museum we began with a concept and image sketch of flying fruit seeds that had just landed on the ground. These shapes, like rolling dewdrops on a lotus leaf, were then translated into glass domes – natural shapes that express the balance between gravity and the surface tension present in a water drop. Water ripples produced by the wind and other water metaphors became a model for the architecture. It may be said that the competition model for the Niigata project is an extension of this imagery, taking the form of seven water droplets.

The Public Character of the Waterfront

I believe that waterfront spaces have a great deal of potential as a model for public space. Japan is a long continuous island chain divided in the middle by high mountains, and the water-ways that flow from these mountains to the sea have historically been at the origin of human settlement, particularly where they meet the ocean. Such geographically complex areas clearly exhibit the change of seasons (spring flowers, autumn foliage, the long days and clement weather of the summer) and became a natural choice for human settlement, public life and, subsequently, art. Over time, a strong relationship between the waterfront and people developed. Water itself is, in one sense, the cultural root of these regions.

Niigata, originally a series of floating islands located at the mouth of the Shinano River, is one such 'water' city; the physical changes in this area have a direct connection with the cultural history of the city. Once an important port connecting Northern Japan to the rest of the world, Niigata had relatively early contact with foreign cultures. When the city was still young, the area at the mouth of the Shinano River was an archipelago: water canals connected the streets to each other and to the river and ocean, and willow trees lined the streets. Niigata was a port city immersed in and surrounded by the fluctuating rhythms of nature. However, as it modernised, much of this character was lost. Canals were gradually filled in to become roads, and by the beginning of the Showa Era (the 1920s), the site of our project had also begun to undergo landfill operations. In view of this history, our initial concept – to establish a green archipelago on the site – was a return to the original landscape of Niigata's waterfront. By re-creating this latent scenery (where Niigata's culture originally thrived), we hoped to stimulate a similar sense of public feeling at our new centre for the performing arts. We also felt that this 'archipelago system' was not just a model for developing this particular site, but could be repeated and extended as a system for revitalising the entire city of Niigata.

Floating Green Gardens

One of the major challenges of the competition was the prohibition of below grade space (despite the extensive parking and infrastructure requirements that threatened to cover the

entire site with paving). Another competition challenge was the incorporation of existing structures on the site into the planned facilities. Given these two conditions, we developed our initial concept (a return to Niigata's primordial landscape) into a series of mid-air gardens, connecting these and the lobbies of the existing buildings on the second level with a network of slopes and bridges. At ground level (below the gardens), parking spaces and trees are arranged in a loose grid pattern. Taken together, the combination of elements reads as a new suspended ground plane in the midst of a green, forest-like atmosphere.

Again in line with the natural theme of the project the mid-air gardens are supported by tree-like structural columns. These gardens connect to the lobbies of the surrounding buildings to create the flowing circulation system of down-town Niigata, through the site, all the way to the Shinano River. The floating gardens were created in the image of *harrapa* (a Japanese term meaning field or empty space), but can also support special open-air performances and other functions. There is an outdoor stage enveloped by a gradually descending spiral slope, a shimmering water stage that per-ceptually overlaps with the surface of the Shinano River, a floating pavilion for springtime flower viewing, and an open area with benches for children.

Architecture as a curtain
The main structure of the Performing Arts Centre consists of three separate halls – a concert stage, a dramatic arts theatre, and a Japanese Noh theatre wrapped in a light transparent membrane. During the competition phase, we considered giving each of the three halls a separate volumetric identity and site, but opted instead to consolidate them in a single package to facilitate new crossover possibilities. Combinations of orchestra with Noh theatre, Japanese Budoh dance with modern dance, Japanese traditional music with Western classical music, Kabuki theatre with opera, art with drama – all are possible as a result of the close proximity of the halls.

Three different scenes of a single opera can be staged in each of the three separate venues – an impossible task with a more dispersed siting strategy.

Niigata is a sake and rice producing region and, as is typical of agricultural regions in Japan, retains many local drama and storytelling traditions. Also, as an active port, Niigata's culture and education have been influenced by outside ideas for many years, resulting in numerous amateur and youth orches-tras, and other Western music performance groups. We thought it important to take advantage of this unique local culture by creating a place where traditional and contem-porary, amateur and professional, and local and international groups could work together. Again, the hope was to create a facility that would promote crossovers and collaborations previously unrealised in such a setting.

The lobby of the main building is, like the other nearby facilities, at the second level. It was designed to be like a public park – a 360 degree, twenty-four hour, fully accessible free space, extended onto various interior levels by stairs, ramps and bridges. An information centre, café, restaurants, practice rooms, gallery, viewing platform, and roof garden are located at various points along this public sequence. Because Niigata has a relatively cold climate, the lobby is enclosed with a high-tech double glazing system. Between the two layers of glass are more layers of perforated aluminium panels that move and overlap to adjust to varying weather conditions. A specially developed sensor system monitors exterior light and air conditions and controls the air conditioning and interior lighting systems in order to lower running costs. Five elliptical mirrors in the lobby multiply the lighting effects and serve an important role in its conception as a communication space. Reflecting people's movements and gatherings and the fluctuating light that passes through the exterior membrane, the mirrors re-present the interior scene to other parts of the building, and even to the exterior (via pro-jections onto the membrane skin). An ever-changing exterior image for the buildings in thus created.

waterfront spaces have a great deal of potential as a model for public space

"Such geographically complex areas clearly exhibit the change of seasons (spring flowers, autumn foliage, the long days and clement weather of the summer) and became a natural choice for human settlement, public life and, sub-sequently, art. Over time, a strong relationship between the waterfront and people developed. Water itself is, in one sense, the cultural route of these regions.

Public Theatre

Each region of Japan still maintains its own traditions and local culture, intimately related to the region's climate and the people's lifestyle. Unlike commercial theatre (which must bring in a certain number of users and create a profit to stay in business), public theatre should not be separated from this local culture. In Niigata we aimed to create a place where people would gather spontaneously – public in the truest sense of the word – and modified the programme accordingly. In the case of the 900-seat dramatic arts theatre, we felt that it was important to consider what kind of theatre would be most actively used in the Niigata context. Although a prosce-nium arch stage (similar to a German opera house) was proposed in the competition brief, we suggested a multi-purpose stage (appropriate even for regional Japanese tradi-tional dance or modern dance), and a movable proscenium that could accommodate a wide variety of performances. We also designed other infrastructure elements – traps, runways, orchestra pits, floor materials, cabling, lighting systems – to be fully flexible, while still fully maintaining professional and industry standards. The result is a theatre that is as suitable for Japanese Kabuki as it is for a full opera. As part of this design process, theatre technology and drama experts often came to our office for meetings and an exchange of information. Through these long and intense sessions, we learned that there had not previously been many opportunities for Western and Japanese professionals to work together in this way; the result was the development of a completely different kind of dramatic theory. Though this kind of exchange is exactly the opposite process of design development for most public halls, it is my hope that the process moves more in this direction in the future.

> I hope to create an architecture incorporating the fluctuations and flowing processes of everyday life – environments that change with and adapt to the changes in our lives

In the case of the 2,000-seat concert arena, we were concerned that the large size might inhibit good acoustic performance, and proposed a smaller programme. Though unsuccessful in reducing the seating capacity, we did reduce the hall's overall volume and therefore were able to control reverberation and other acoustic properties more carefully. This main hall is fully equipped to accommodate any number of performances, from full opera to highly specialised musical performances. The opening performance *Ocean* (Merce Cunningham and John Cage's final collaboration) is one example of an effective utilisation of the arena's unique capabilities. The Noh theatre was also designed to be highly flexible; many of the traditional stage elements are removable, and the space can even be naturally lit from a nearby courtyard. With these transformable stage and lighting arrangements, it is possible to utilise this space for Japanese Budoh dance, the tea ceremony, flower arrange-ment, Japanese traditional music, or even modern dance. In response to requests from the local residents, the music pit of the Noh stage can be used as a tea ceremony space or for large and small gatherings.

Inclusive Mind

Public architecture is valuable only if it is well used and fosters regional culture and learning. Currently, elected officials are expected to represent a wide variety of users when developing public architecture – but as society has become more complex, this representation has become increasingly outdated: I believe it is necessary to create a system of partnership between the public administration and the public itself, through a combination of programming and planning/ management workshops. As opposed to the current system (where select administrators present decisions already taken), a more participatory process is needed. Such a process, I believe, would lead to changing inspirations and lifestyles, and a shift in our cultural development and education.

In order to create public space that is truly in tune with the life of local residents, it is imperative to have places where diverse interests can openly interact. I believe that archi-tecture is intimately related to living culture, that program-matic flexibility is critical to the establishment of environ-ments adaptable to the coming age, and that the truly democratic involvement of local residents is critical to creating such public space. If there is free participation in the making of architecture, public space can really take on the task of improving human life.

Architecture as programming

Architecture is intimately related to life – from its initial planning through to its post construction management – and the process of creating architecture has enormous potential. In our experience, the public administration of each locale is very different, and we have accordingly taken very different approaches to our various projects. Also, we have witnessed a wide range of grass-roots participation within various administrations. Generally, we try to see the various occu-pations and societal roles of the local community residents – shop owners, school teachers, office workers, etc. – in terms of their specialised interests, skills, or expertise. Even future users – grade school, junior and senior high school students – have wide-ranging and important opinions. Rather than listening to a select group of representatives, we have found that meeting and involving all these people face to face is the best way to establish trust. To do this, it is critical to have a non-hierarchical organisational structure. Rather than a process dominated by experts, we aim for a think-tank environment, responsive to local ideas, that incorporates frequent presentations of the design. Organising symposia and recruiting staff members from the local population is an important part of this process.

With this attitude, genuinely participatory workshops become possible, and architecture and programming come to have an intimate relationship (since planning, management,

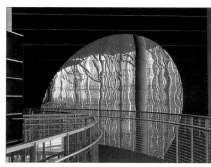

PAGES 42-43: Niigata landscape
RIGHT: Niigata Performing Arts Centre, Traditional Noh theatre Photograph, Mitsumasa Fujitsuka
MIDDLE: Concert hall Photograph, Katsuhisa Kida
FAR RIGHT: Interior Photograph, Mitsumasa Fujitsuka

support groups, volunteers, guests, and local experts are working together towards shared goals). Even after construction begins there should be continued dialogue with the community – a way for groups to take tours, and for local universities to use the construction site as a learning resource for students. These processes, and all the other processes that go into making a building, should be recorded and distributed on the internet. In order to create a place that is loved by the local people, traces of their participation should be evident. Architecture begins with a concept, but exists within a process. Public architecture must incorporate people's lifestyle and be a place that continuously challenges and activates the consciousness of the people; participation by all is essential.

In the case of Niigata, we created and ran the N-PAC Workshop (Niigata Performing Arts Centre Workshop) for three years. Born from an idea shared by the Administration that architecture should not be separated from programming, this workshop trained the planning staff of the new facility and studied public hall management issues and the establishment of a 'network' of public facilities. The focus of activity was on public lectures concerning a wide variety of topics. These helped us to learn about local opinions, and to create a new audience for the planned facility. The lecturers (over one hundred in three years) were all very active in their respective fields. I personally participated in all the various meetings (writing texts, lecturing and attending lectures, acting in workshops, and leading round table discussions) – in short, experiencing and learning together with the N-PAC staff and local people.

Archipelago

An exhibition of our work at the NAI (Netherlands Architecture Institute) in Rotterdam and an installation we designed at the nearby Boyman's Museum had as their common theme 'archipelago,' a term that describes the diverse vectors tested by our projects. 'Inclusive mind' is another term that might be used to describe this approach. Among the many factors that

account for architecture, we believe an 'archipelagic' or 'inclusive' process accounts for various project conditions, the complicated and varied opinions of people, the plurality of relationships involved in architecture, etc. Conceptualising architecture in this way is therefore akin to island hopping, a non-linear, eccentric way of thinking – in a certain sense overlapping the way information is exchanged on the internet.

Process City

Fundamental to the notion of a 'process city' is my belief that buildings are part of a long and changing continuum well after they are first conceived, designed, and built. As such, an inclusive, multi-layered approach to design is essential. While the city has its own irregularities and a built-in sense of chaos, I believe it has still undeveloped potential for even more of this positive fluctuation. In particular, waterfront areas have an abundance of ever-shifting winds and tides that are comforting because they resonate with human and musical rhythms. Ultimately, architecture and the city also work with these rhythms; therefore, it is necessary to incorporate natural cycles in the creation of new places.

Fluctuation is a concept incorporating notions of freedom and dissipation. Like the never ending, indeterminate process of living in the city, it is impossible to forecast. Our research on the 'process city' points to an architecture that incorporates the collective memories and latent nature of the city, as well as the open possibilities of flexible, empty space. The rapid ageing of society should be considered in these terms – how can it be mobilised to create a softer, feminine, and more positive environment. Along with these more conceptual notions, the 'process city' should also consider water usage, planting, and other ecological factors in order to both preserve and create nature. I hope to create an architecture incorporating the fluctuations and flowing processes of everyday life – environments that change with and adapt to the changes in our lives.

'Island hopping' implies a choice of paths, connections, and disconnections – a freedom that I am striving to incorporate into my architecture. Translated into landscape, it might be interpreted in the guise of floating green islands, or archipelagos.

The process of making architecture is likened to an archipelago, an eccentric island pattern. It is a poetic act, similar in spirit to the composition and performance of music.

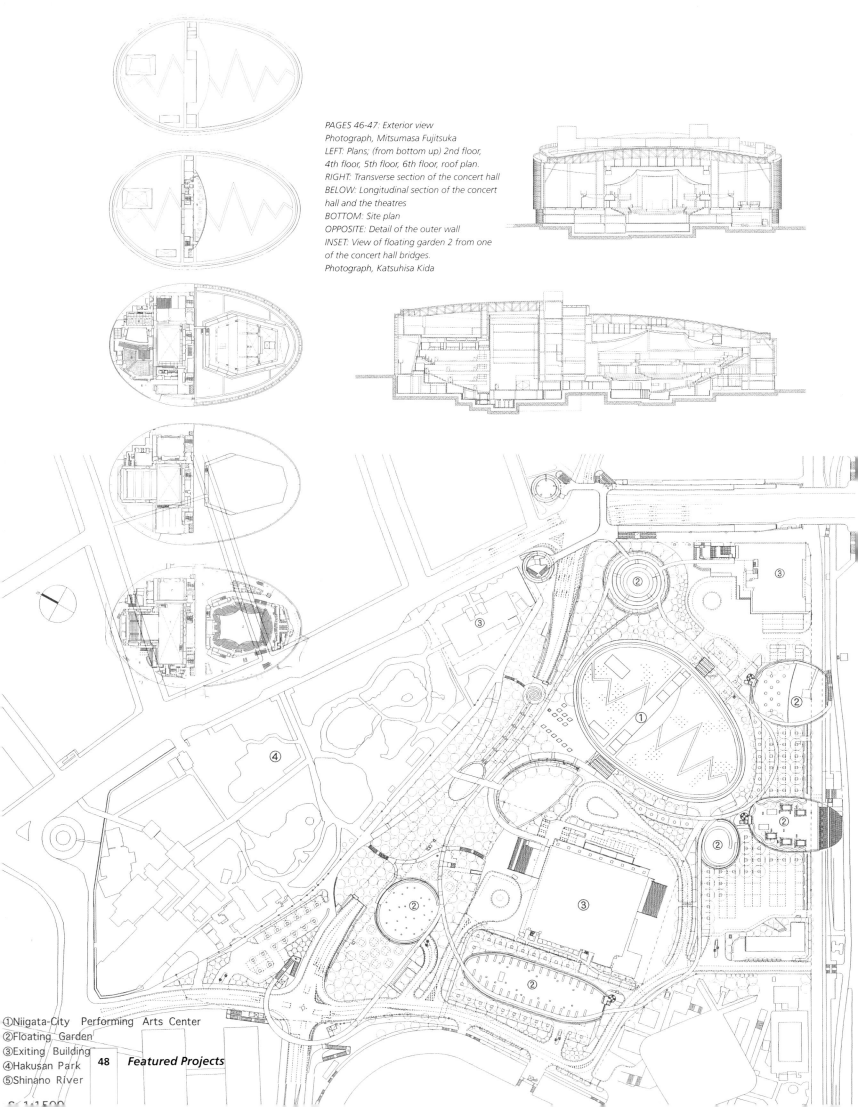

PAGES 46-47: Exterior view
Photograph, Mitsumasa Fujitsuka
LEFT: Plans; (from bottom up) 2nd floor,
4th floor, 5th floor, 6th floor, roof plan.
RIGHT: Transverse section of the concert hall
BELOW: Longitudinal section of the concert
hall and the theatres
BOTTOM: Site plan
OPPOSITE: Detail of the outer wall
INSET: View of floating garden 2 from one
of the concert hall bridges.
Photograph, Katsuhisa Kida

①Niigata-City Performing Arts Center
②Floating Garden
③Exiting Building
④Hakusan Park   **48   Featured Projects**
⑤Shinano River

Eight Concepts

No fixed platform exists for the museum; the site is therefore continuous and overlaps with the entire developing area.

The process of creating art becomes a part of the exhibition, a work of art in itself.

The museum is integrated with nature; nature becomes part of the museum.

The museum will not have a permanent collection at the first stage.

Free circulation helps create freedom of programming and exhibiting.

The museum will exhibit virtual installations of 20th century Mexican art utilising multimedia image projections.

The museum is also a place for meditation and relaxation.

The museum is open-ended; it will be engendered and recreated continuously .

Toyo Ito

JVC contemporary art, design and architecture

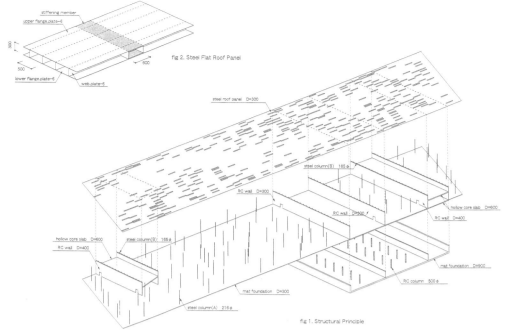

fig 2. Steel Flat Roof Panel

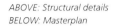

fig 1. Structural Principle

We consider the whole environment as the museum and believe that architecture is a part of nature. By casting a roof in nature, spaces are generated. Three spaces are created by this method. The temporary exhibition space will embody eight concepts. In the current scheme, the descriptions of each space are as follows.

ABOVE: Structural details
BELOW: Masterplan

MASTERPLAN 1/800

Temporary Exhibition Space

The space will mainly be arranged for temporary exhibitions on travel, and will employ a highly flexible exhibition system using movable partitions. There will be two exhibition rooms: a small one; and a big one to house large-scale works. To meet the airconditioning requirements for temporary exhibitions, the walls will be made of concrete equipped with adequate thermal insulation and dehumidifying material for interior finishing. In order to conserve energy, the south facing wall will be doubled, with the aim of storing energy in the construction.

Media Installation Space

Large murals, images, and 20th-century Mexican paintings will be the nucleus. For media installations, blind screens fixed in the double glazing on three planes of the wall will appear, and images will be projected onto them from projectors suspended from the ceiling. The images will also be projected onto the pond that comes in from outside giving the audience the impression that they are in the space in the murals while they recline on comfortable chairs around the pond. At other times, the pond is observed through the glazing, creating a relaxing environment.

Outdoor Exhibition Space

Artists will be invited to the outdoor exhibition space of the museum on a regular basis. They will establish there workshops, sculpting demonstrations, and the installation of temporary exhibitions.

This will permit the creation of artworks not only under the roof but also towards the plaza, the garden, and the extension of the museum. The resulting artworks will be under cover in specially constructed sheds.

The museum and the plaza in front of it can be combined to create a setting for for outdoor functions and events.

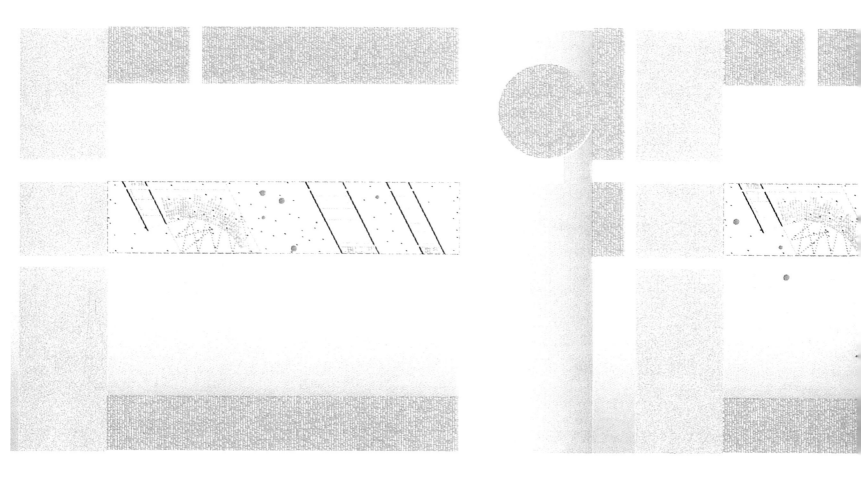

*The process of creating a work of art becomes part of
the exhibition, a work of art in itself*

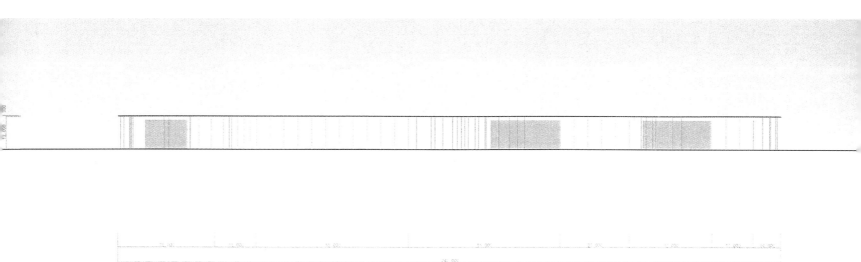

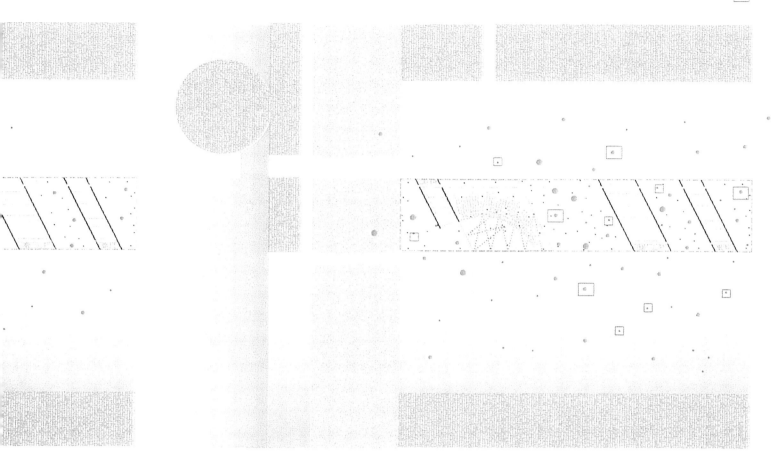

The exhibition area will change continuously and grow over time.
The museum is open-ended.
It will be engendered and recreated continuously.

World Stadium Team

Foster and Partners, HOK Lobb

The New Wembley Stadium

It is a triumphant arch. In the spirit of any team, we have sought to push back the limits to generate an improved performance

Lord Foster

With capacity figures exceeding the requirements of the National Lottery, the new Wembley Stadium is the centrepiece of England's bid for the 2006 World Cup.

The famous twin towers are being replaced with a spectacular 133m high arch that will tower over the 52m high 90,000-seat stadium providing a dramatic landmark and framing the view of the stadium from the walk up Olympic Way towards the main façade. The elimination of the four masts in favour of the single arch allows for a larger and completely uninterrupted public concourse around the north entrance. A 2,000-seat Banqueting Hall with a public viewing terrace punctuates the front façade.

The sliding roof remains an integral part of the design for the new stadium. Wembley's pitch is famous as one of the finest in the world. Maintaining this quality while designing a new stadium that is considerably taller than the existing building, and placing fans closer to the pitch has been a key challenge for the design team. Computer models have allowed the team to track air movement and sunlight on the existing pitch and a unique sliding roof has been developed to create optimum viewing conditions in the new stadium. The roof will be left open between events but can be moved to line up with the touchline within 15 minutes, ensuring that every spectator is under cover during an event. An athletics track will be constructed only as needed, thus ensuring that spectators for all events will be sitting as close to the action as possible.

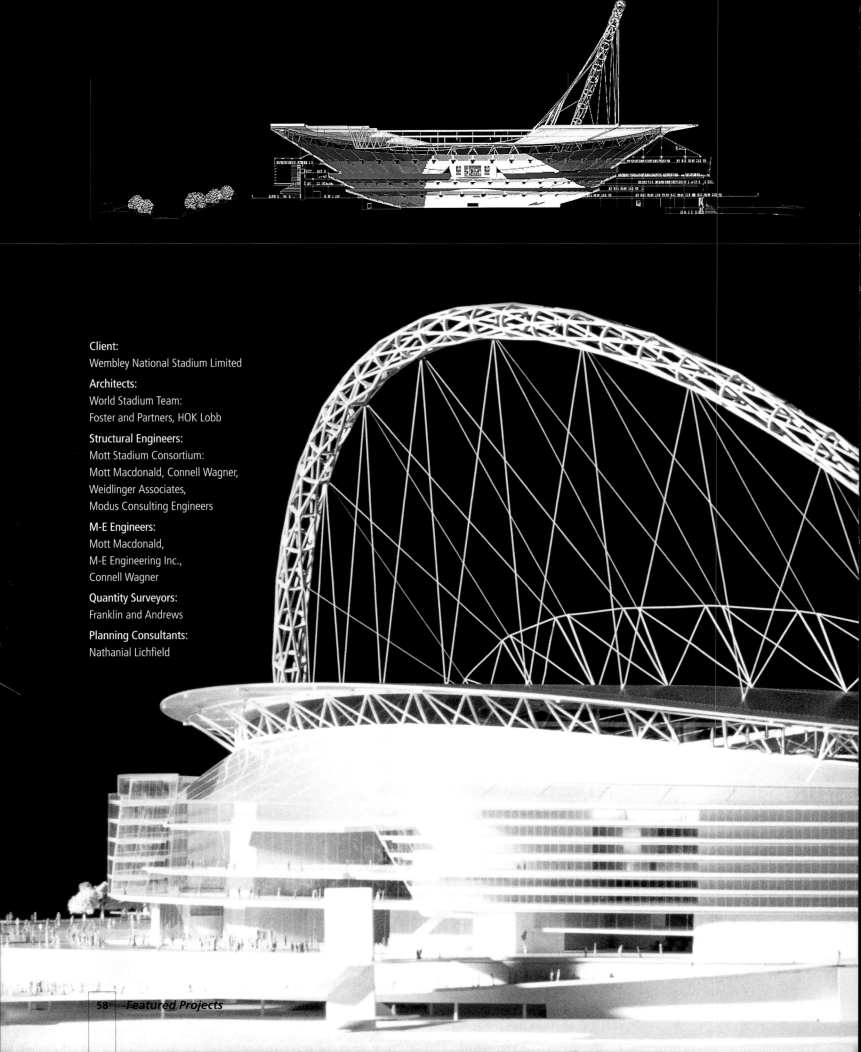

Client:
Wembley National Stadium Limited

Architects:
World Stadium Team:
Foster and Partners, HOK Lobb

Structural Engineers:
Mott Stadium Consortium:
Mott Macdonald, Connell Wagner,
Weidlinger Associates,
Modus Consulting Engineers

M-E Engineers:
Mott Macdonald,
M-E Engineering Inc.,
Connell Wagner

Quantity Surveyors:
Franklin and Andrews

Planning Consultants:
Nathanial Lichfield

PAGES 56-57: CAD visualisation of the new stadium
Image, GMJ
OPPOSITE ABOVE: Cross section
Foster and Partners visualisation
BELOW: Model
Photograph, Nigel Young/Foster and Partners
ABOVE: Long section
Foster and Partners visualisation

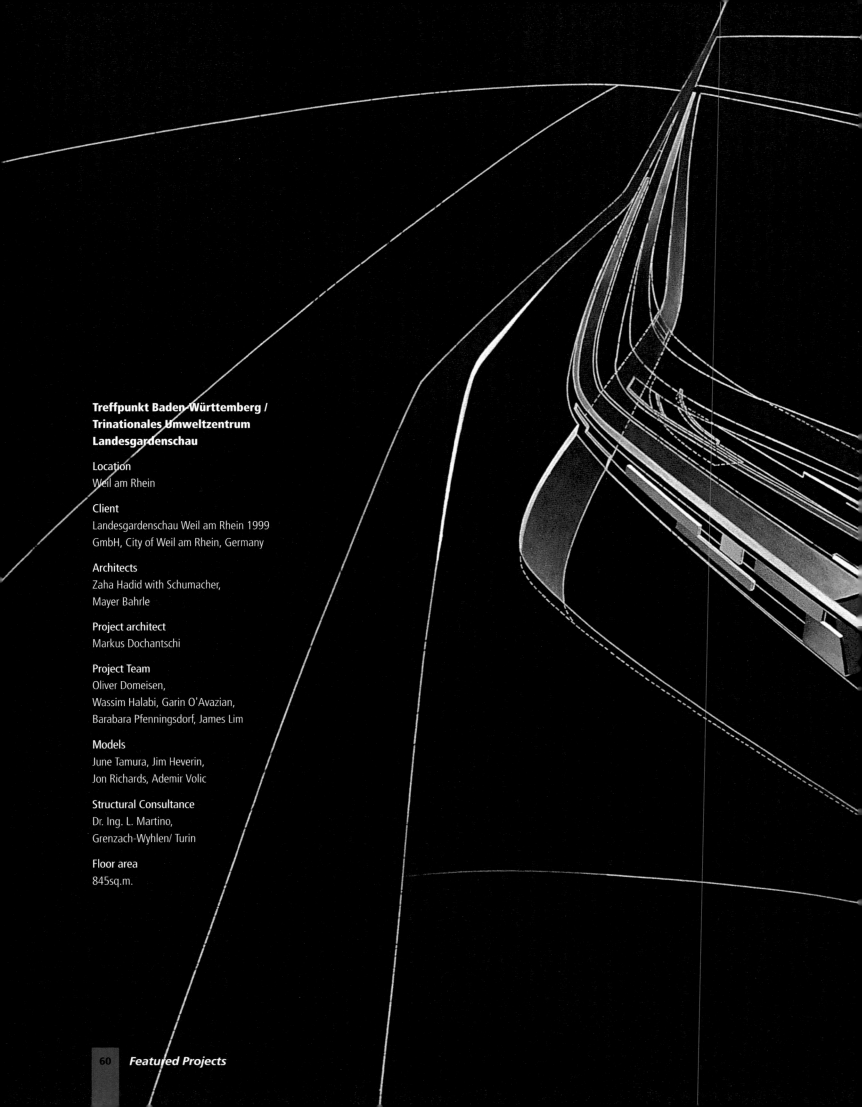

**Treffpunkt Baden-Württemberg /
Trinationales Umweltzentrum
Landesgardenschau**

Location
Weil am Rhein

Client
Landesgardenschau Weil am Rhein 1999
GmbH, City of Weil am Rhein, Germany

Architects
Zaha Hadid with Schumacher,
Mayer Bahrle

Project architect
Markus Dochantschi

Project Team
Oliver Domeisen,
Wassim Halabi, Garin O'Avazian,
Barabara Pfenningsdorf, James Lim

Models
June Tamura, Jim Heverin,
Jon Richards, Ademir Volic

Structural Consultance
Dr. Ing. L. Martino,
Grenzach-Wyhlen/ Turin

Floor area
845sq.m.

Zaha Hadid

LF one, Weil am Rhein

ABOVE LEFT: Interior detail. Photograph, Christian Richters. ABOVE RIGHT: View from north-east. Photograph, Hélène Binet. BACKGROUND: General perspective

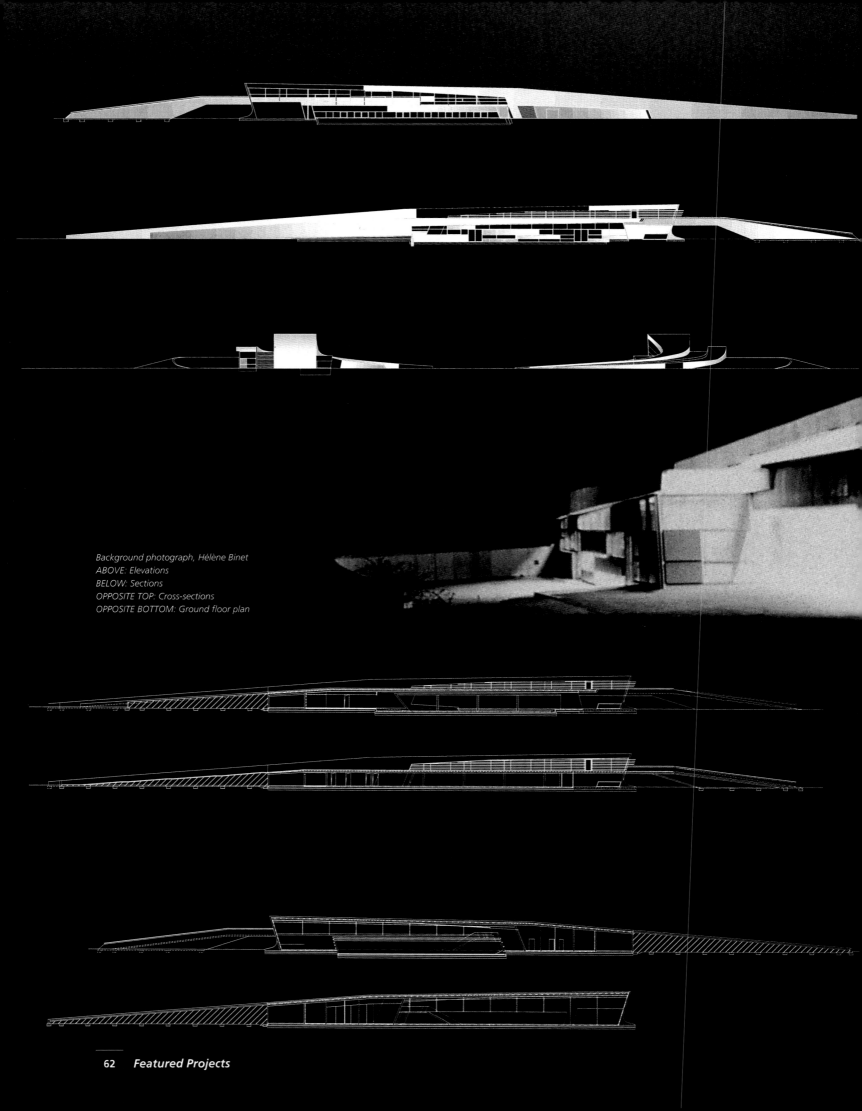

Background photograph, Hélène Binet
ABOVE: Elevations
BELOW: Sections
OPPOSITE TOP: Cross-sections
OPPOSITE BOTTOM: Ground floor plan

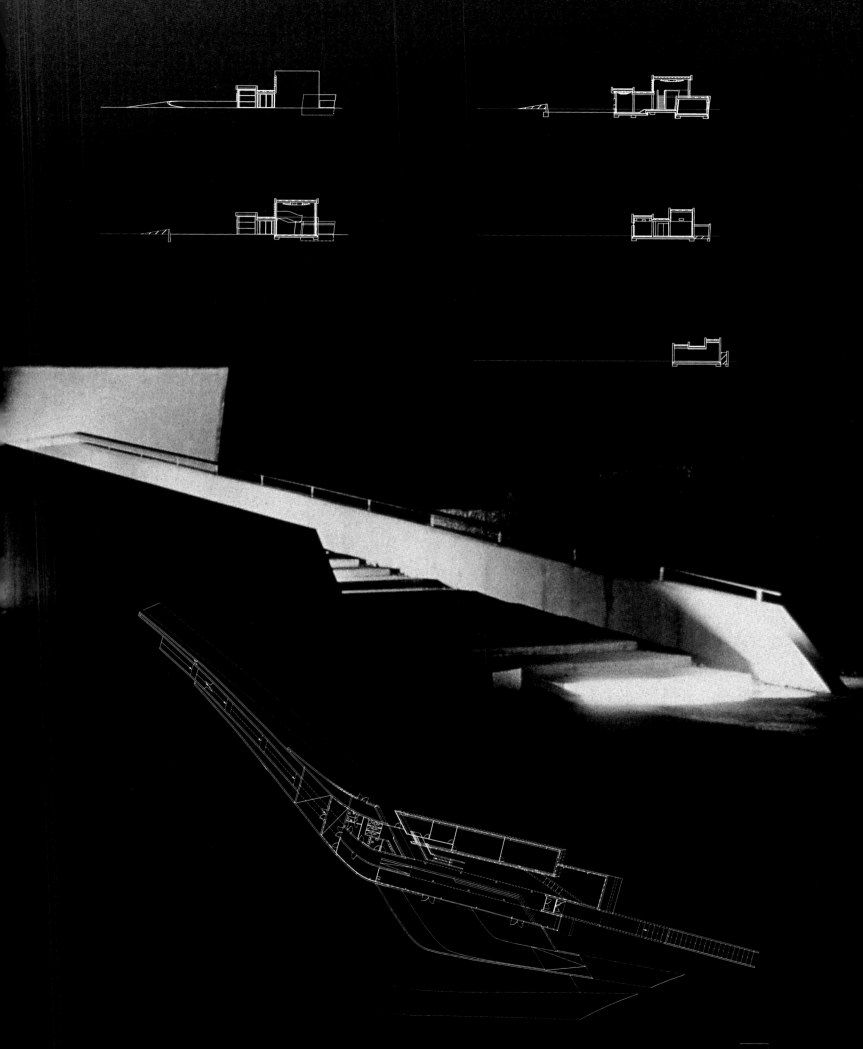

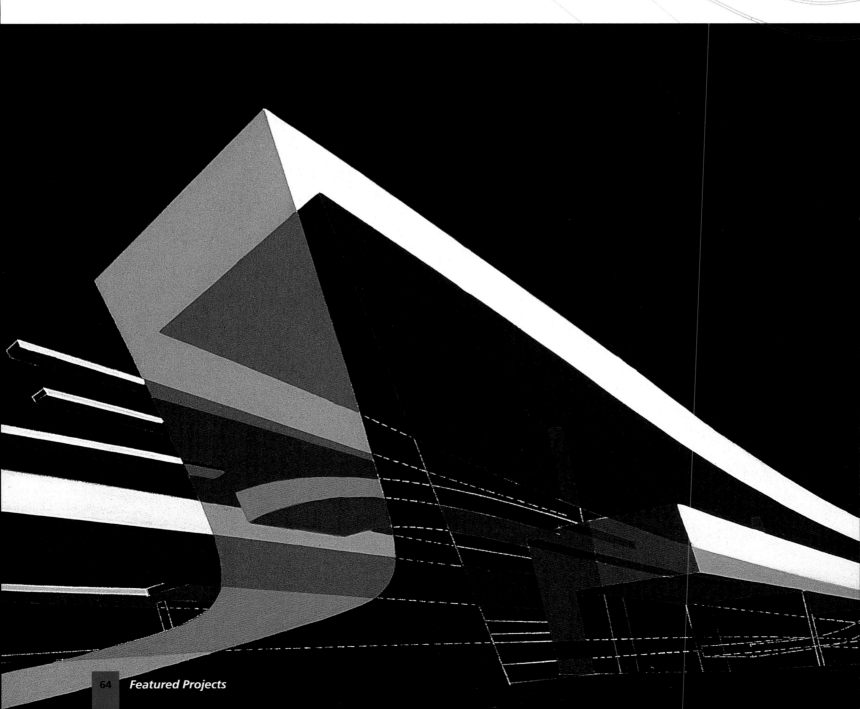

The exhibition building for the landscape and gardening show is conceived in terms of landscape features rather than in terms of geometric order.

The smooth concrete structure emerges from the fluid geometry of the surrounding network of paths. Three of those paths entangle to make the building. Four parallel, partly interwoven spaces are caught in this bundle of paths. One path snuggles up to the south side of the building, another, gently slopping, rises over its back, whereas the third path cuts diagonally through the interior. The main spaces, exhibition hall and café stretch along those routes and allow for plenty of sunlight and views from the exterior. Secondary rooms 'disappear' within the 'root' of the building.

The building generates and integrates a series of outdoor spaces, like the café terrace on the south side. Its smooth geometry extends into the surroundings, inventing new artificial shapes and landforms. The centre for environmental research is situated north of the exhibition hall; half submerged into the ground in order to take advantage of the isolating quality of the earth itself.

The building offers a walk in a garden, a landscape that has been transformed into architecture. The building serves, features, and generated out of the ground.

It finds its place between object and landscape.

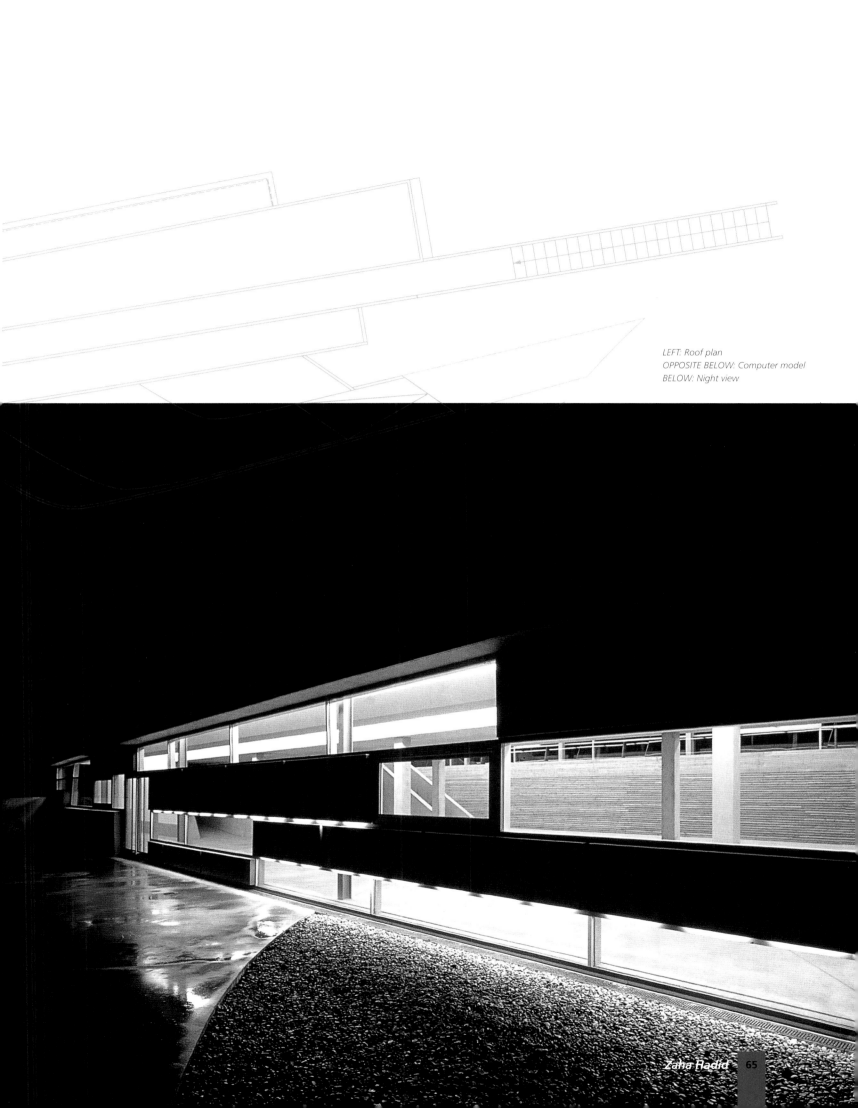

LEFT: Roof plan
OPPOSITE BELOW: Computer model
BELOW: Night view

Philip Johnson

At 94 Philip Johnson, as active as ever, has a number of ongoing projects and is further developing ideas he first used in the Case Western Reserve University. His new buildings incorporate large sculptural elements inspired by medieval buttressing and are full of sensuality. They form the basis of several projects including the Berlin Alternative, and the Gate House and Wayfarers' Chapel at Johnson's estate in Canaan, Connecticut; they further evolved with the Cathedral of Hope in Dallas, Texas.

His modest explanation of these projects is that he "borrows from his friends" (Eisenman and Gehry). He makes no claim to have invented something new – that may or may not be influenced by Derridean deconstruction – but his designs make a significant contribution to a new direction in architecture.

The Gate House

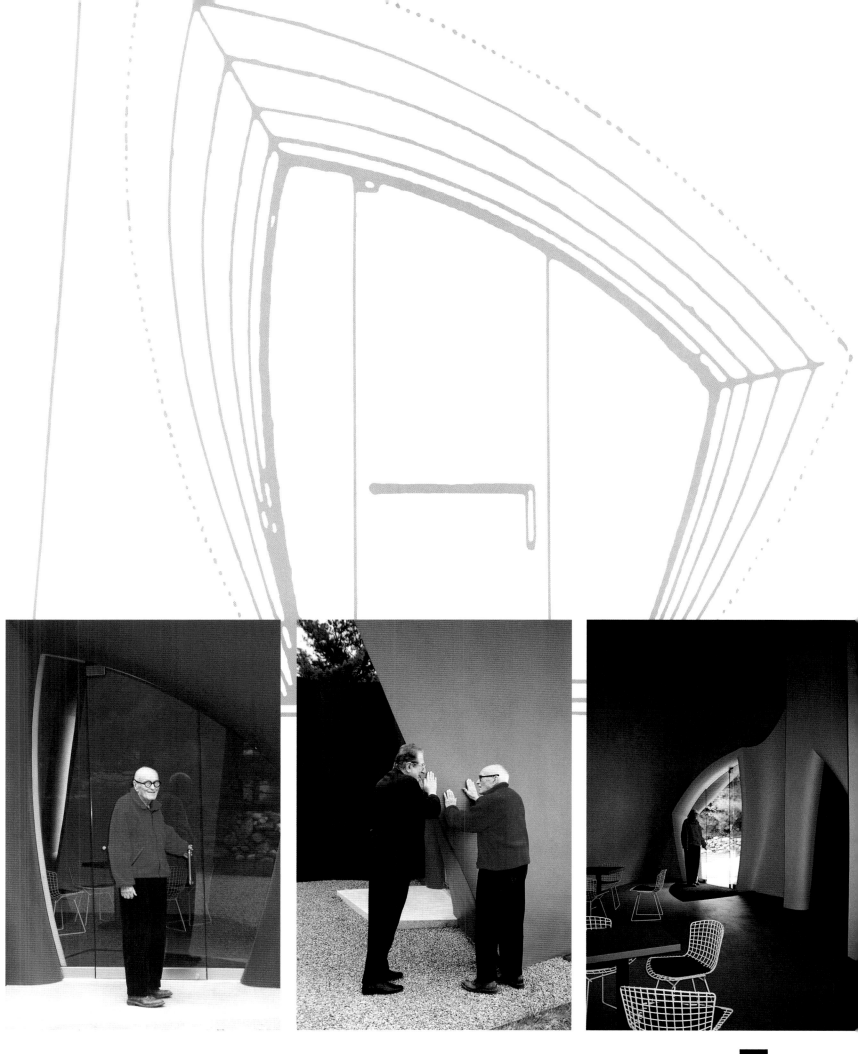

Rockefeller Guesthouse and the Glass House

Built for $75,000 in 1950, acquired for $3.5 million in 1989 by London gallery owner Anthony d'Offay, the Rockefeller Guesthouse has come up for auction at Christie's New York as the epilogue to a sale of "Masterworks: 1900 to 2000," where it sold for $11 million, far in excess of its $3.5 million estimate.

The Guesthouse is built on a sliver of land and has an elongated plan that owes much of its design to the Glass House. In Johnson's words "The sense of space is stretched visually by creating a procession between indoor and outdoor volumes – the plan features a partially covered interior court which is open to the sky, and has a pool of water with stepping stones between two enclosed rooms framed by floor-to-ceiling glass walls." The house was commissioned and originally used by Mrs Blanchette Rockefeller as a showcase for some of her artworks and as a space for entertaining her guests. It was subsequently donated to MOMA and eventually sold privately.

Philip Johnson lived there for a short while: "The only way to live in New York." When asked how it compared with the Glass House on his Canaan estate, he replied, "I have better wallpaper in the country."

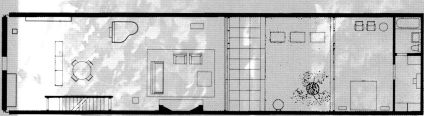

ABOVE: Rockefeller Guesthouse, Plan. OPPOSITE: The Glass House. Photograph, AP-NA. BELOW: Guest House, view of bedroom through the terrace. BACKGROUND: Rockefeller Guesthouse, the terrace and living room in the background. Photographs, Alexander Vethers, courtesy Christie's.

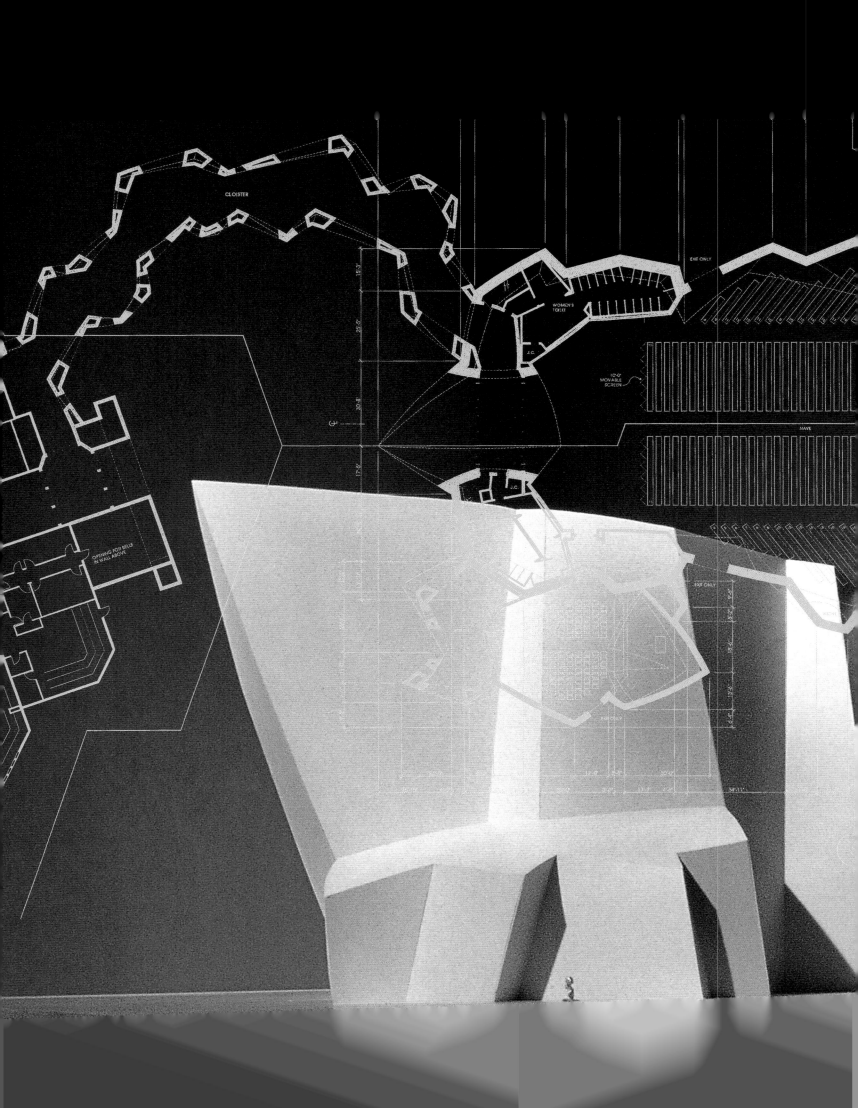

Philip Johnson's Cathedral of Hope

Dimitri Fatouros

The Cathedral of Hope in Dallas, Texas is a cathedral for a predominantly gay congregation. It is to replace an existing church which the community has outgrown. The design redefines the stereotype in such a way that it is concealed: the liturgical processes are transferred and transformed into a built situation based on aspects of modernism with echoes of Louis Kahn. The design concept is a "translation" of buttresses and on folding and unfolding. In medieval buildings buttresses were the result of constructional constraints but their rich play of shadows and hidden connotations make for good design today. Johnson uses them as a means of transformation and as a symbolic geometry for the exterior and for the interior void, which he reorganises and transforms into a spatial *cosmos* of his own. There is continuity throughout, resonant of the low voice of diachronicity. The internal differentiations enhance the feeling of space, organise various spatial situations, and recall a multiplicity of spatio-visual events.

There is a studied asymmetry. The entrance elements, the arrangement of the seats and the micro visual field surrounding them all differentiate the symmetries. The axis deviates from the conventional: there is a door on one side; but the expected door on the other side is not there. The wall near the staircases picks up the small wall in the background.

The portico (*stoa*) is an important element of a cathedral. Here it has been transformed from its origins to become almost a contradiction of the *raison d'être* of a portico. Johnson's

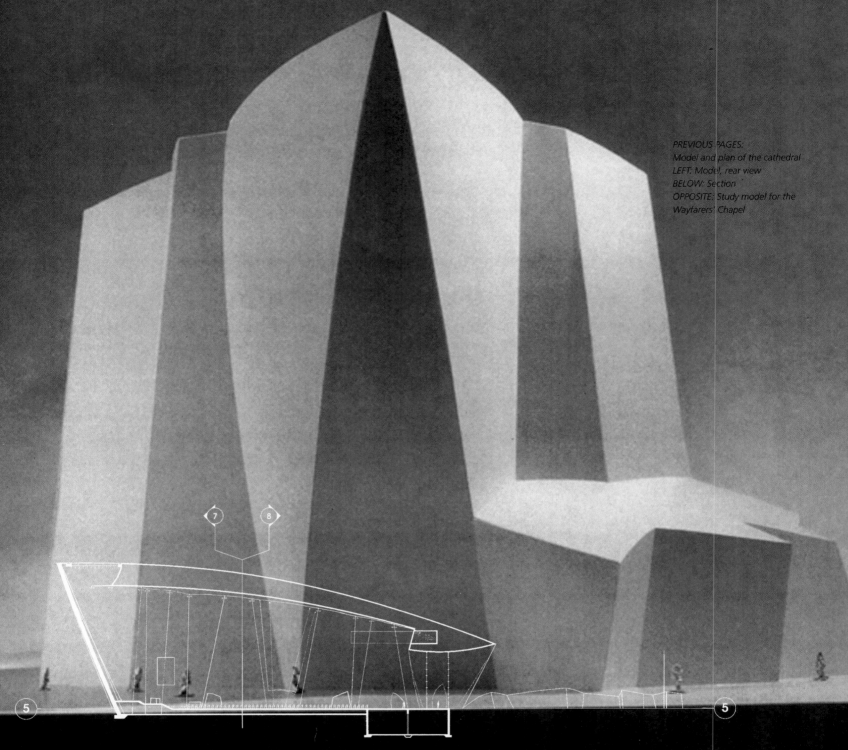

PREVIOUS PAGES:
Model and plan of the cathedral
LEFT: Model, rear view
BELOW: Section
OPPOSITE: Study model for the
Wayfarers' Chapel

design uses the type in a way that leads to a new understanding of the type. This is true not only of the overall scale of the work but also of the interior, where he transforms a void into space.

The non rectilinear is organised into a multi-complex erotic and sensual place. The relationships of sharp and soft, curvilinear and rectilinear forms make it a typical expressionistic work that recalling Charoun and Mendelsohn's timid curvilinear approach.

The shape reflects the envelope I do not want to use the word wall since wall refers only to construction and this is not a reading of architecture based on construction methods and achievements. It is about creating space from voids. It may be an exaggeration to say that architecture is not about construction but in fact architecture uses construction but is not a translation of construction. It is the will to create space.

A work of architecture is always *non finito*; it is part of the process that brings a multilevel, multilateral richness to human situations. This Cathedral is not merely part of this trend but a dramatic step forward.

Philip Johnson is a master architect and a complicated one: his work is much richer than it at first appears. He modestly claims to copy his friends, referring especially to Eisenman and Gehry, but, of course, he does not but he reminds us that creative architecture does make use of the concepts of the masters and of anonymous works.

Today it is becoming more and more difficult for architecture to induce people to feel at ease, to experience sensuality, to carry on a dialogue. Neither architecture nor the arts now play an important role in the struggle against barbarism; they do not affect our well being although they may provide moments of hope, which is important on a personal level. But where does architecture stand in the battle for a less aggressive world? Even the Cathedral of Hope can only moderate the stresses faced by its congregation but it does express another way of thinking, another way of life.

Atelier Hollein

Location:
St. Ours-les-Roches, Auvergne, France

Client:
Conseil Régional d'Auvergne,
Clermont-Ferrand

Project team:
Hans Hollein, Architect/Design principal
Hans-Peter Wunsch, Project leader

Associated architects / Supervision:
Atelier 4, Clermont Ferrand
(Project Coordinator, Philippe Tixier)

Consultants:
BET ITC (Structural Engineers), BET
Choulet (Mechanical/HVAC), Geoconsult
Ingenieurgemeinschaft (Geological
Consultants), Rainer Verbizh (Scenography),
Michel Forgue (Economist), CAPRI
ACOUSTIQUE (Acoustical), Lichtdesign
Ingenieurs g.m.b.H. (Lighting), Acanthe
(Landscape architects)

Photographs:
Studio Hollein / Arch. Sina Baniahmad

Hans Hollein

Vulcania
European Centre of Volcanism

BACKGROUND: Model, general view
ABOVE: Section

The Centre and Museum of Volcanism relate to man's curiosity and search for knowledge but also to the strong emotions evoked by life and death, by the creation of the earth and the birth of humanity. Atavistic feelings are reflected in the ambivalence of our attraction to fire as both a constructive and destructive force. Volcanoes are a constant reminder of the ongoing process of the formation of our planet.

There is a strongly ritualistic and symbolic aspect about the idea of a centre of volcanism, an idea strengthened by the choice of site – not in a city but in a natural area with the strong visual presence of volcanic activity and where extinct volcanoes dominate.

The location of the site, completely isolated in a natural landscape at an altitude of almost 1000m in an area of visually present extinct volcanoes with their characteristic shapes demands that any building be integrated with nature. In addition, the theme strongly supports a subterranean development.

Architecturally, this concept is truly three-dimensional. It is both subtractive and additive and allows for the free development of spaces and movement in any direction: horizontally, vertically and diagonally. The European Centre of Volcanism has both scientific and

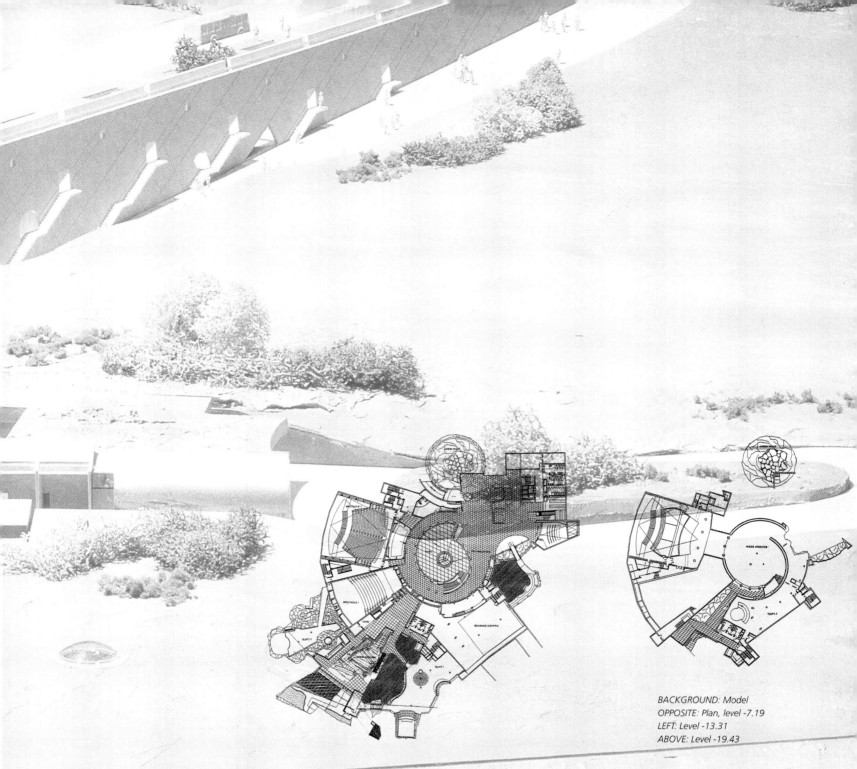

BACKGROUND: Model
OPPOSITE: Plan, level -7.19
LEFT: Level -13.31
ABOVE: Level -19.43

emotional implications. The museum must attract visitors with differing interests, differing ages and from different educational backgrounds. A visit to the Centre should be both educational and enjoyable. The spatial and visual arrangements of the site and buildings – both above and below ground – must relay the message of volcanism on an emotional and educational level.

The building is a reason to visit the Auvergne: it is specific to its singular situation, is memorable and clearly identifiable. It speaks about volcanoes both directly and metaphorically. There is no separation between building and landscape or between container and content, either underground or on the surface. A processional path leads down into an abyss towards the centre of the Earth, reminiscent of Jules Verne and Dante's purgatory; but it is also a reference to the womb and to the protective cave. Fire is present, symbolizing magma and the life that springs from it. The atmosphere can be sinister and threatening but also exuberant and joyful. Ashes contrast with nature. The Centre celebrates the Auvergne's links with volcanism and nature. It is an area rich in volcanic traces of great beauty creating a special atmosphere. The materials of the Centre derive from the nature of the site – stone, grass, water.

When the visitor climbs back to the surface he will have a grandiose view of the region and of Puy-de-Dôme. Confronted by the imposing presence of the Auvergne volcanoes, he will be drawn by all the volcanic objects and products around him, from the mineral water on the dining table to the stones used for building the magnificent Auvergnate churches.

ABOVE: Cone interior
OPPOSITE: Model view of access ramp

Site area:
570,000 sq.m / 6,133,200 sq.ft

Total floor area:
16,151 sq.m / 173,784 sq.ft

Exhibition area:
Foyer / Vestibule:
1,468 sq.m / 17,732 sq.ft
Cinemas:
970 sq.m / 10,437 sq.ft
Restaurants / Café:
939 sq.m / 10,103 sq.ft
Office / Lab / Conference rooms:
1,670 sq.m / 17,969 sq.ft
Other:
6,404 sq.m / 68,907 sq.ft

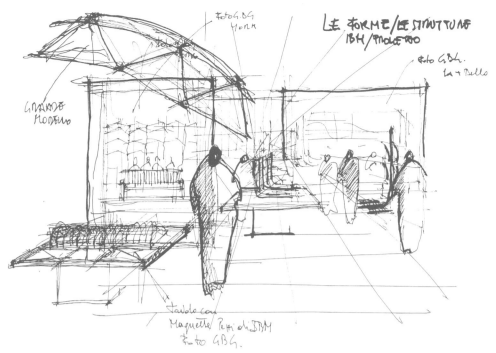

Renzo Piano

Un Regard Construit

A Builder's Gaze

OPPOSITE ABOVE: Concept sketch for the installation of the exhibition "Renzo Piano, Un Regard Construit" at the Pompidou Centre. BELOW: Views of the exhibition. Photographs, M. Denancé.

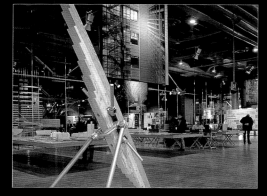

Twenty-five years after it was designed by Piano and Rogers, the Pompidou Centre is mounting an exhibition on the work and thinking of Renzo Piano. In fact, Piano will be honoured throughout the year 2000 for a number of reasons.

First, there is the recent inauguration of two major projects: the Jean-Marie Tjibaou Cultural Centre in Nouméa; and the Potsdamer Platz in Berlin. Then there is the completion of the total renovation of the interior spaces of the Pompidou itself, including the reworking of the three levels of the main lobby and the terraces. (The Centre had to be closed for two years so that the work could be carried out).

This major exhibition of Piano's work will enable a large public to discover his particular universe. Mounted by Piano himself, it covers 1,500sq.m and presents some twenty projects completed during his thirty-year career, as well as a dozen works never previously shown that are currently under study by the two offices of the Renzo Piano Building Workshop in Paris and Genoa.

A builder at heart, Piano has a predilection for the work site. He himself sees it as an engineering laboratory where the ideas and know-how that constitute the very substance of architecture come together: day by day, each project dictates its own particular kind of research or the amount of patient labour required to see it to fruition.

Other important elements of his work are his passion for materials, his constant quest for new and innovative systems, and his desire to test hypotheses through the systematic creation of prototypes.

Despite the number and size of his current commissions, Piano continues to stress his 'craftsmanlike' approach to

Commenting on the remodelling of the Pompidou Centre, Richard Rogers said:

"Whilst it is a joy to see the façades of the Pompidou Centre restored to their former colourful brilliance, and to see the administration finally removed from valuable gallery space, it is a great sadness to see the two guiding innovations of the Centre abandoned...

The Centre was designed to create total departmental flexibility by removing all vertical movement, structure and servicing elements from the inside to the perimeter leaving large uninterrupted loft spaces. It sought to extend the public domain onto the façade of the building locating all people movement systems in glazed corridors and escalators overlooking the piazza.

It is tragic that these successful strategies have been irreversibly damaged by the introduction in the body of the building of an enclosed vertical shaft housing escalators and lift. This shaft not only disrupts the open flow of floor space but also takes the majority of visitors away from the glazed piazza façade into the depths of the building, dramatically reducing the dynamic interaction between 'people on façade' and 'people on piazza.' To make matters worse this reduction of the public animation is being intensified by the introduction of an entrance fee to the escalators, a previously public space.

These errors risk sucking the energy and youthfulness from Place Beaubourg.

All buildings must change to meet the needs of new generations, but change must be incorporated in harmony with their true nature."

Pompidou Centre

building. Indeed, the exhibition strives to recreate the ambiance, the environment, the enormous amount of work, and the untold research that is involved in each architectural project.

Unlike previous exhibitions – including the one presented in 1998 at the Beyeler Foundation in Basel – "Renzo Piano, a Builder's Gaze" proposes a new reading of the architect's work.

The projects exhibited range from "early works" to works in progress. To avoid the past mistake of relying on a purely chronological and overly methodical approach, this exhibition has been arranged according to three main concepts: invention, the urban setting and the senses. Thus, the projects on display afford the visitor a comprehensive view of the architect's work, cutting across time periods, while at the same time illustrating certain common themes. From more than a hundred completed projects, pride of place has been given to "foundation" works.

Renzo Piano himself designed the layout of the exhibition in the southern gallery of the Pompidou Centre. Twenty-two tables, each measuring 6m by 2m, suspended from the gallery's ceiling by a "forest of cables," create a setting that recalls the architect's particular universe. Two tables are devoted to reading materials, the showing of films and consultation of computer monitors. On the other tables, projects are presented in the form of models and prototypes constructed by the Renzo Piano Building Workshop. Each table is accompanied by large-size photographs

Mounted on the walls are a dozen projects never exhibited before: until recently they were being analysed on the walls of the Piano offices. They include the Tokyo headquarters of Hermès, the offices of *Il Sole 24 Ore* in Milan, the Paul Klee Museum in Bern, a sculpture garden in Dallas, and a new museum for Harvard University in Cambridge, Massachusetts.

The exhibition will also be shown at the National Gallery in Berlin.

OPPOSITE: Views of the remodelled Pompidou Centre.
Photographs, M. Denancé
BACKGROUND: Potsdamer Platz, site plan
BELOW: General view of the Potsdamer Platz development.
Photograph, V. Mosch
RIGHT: View of the Marlene Dietrich Platz, Potsdamer Platz
Photograph, E. Cano
FAR RIGHT: Aerial view of the Potsdamer Platz.
Photograph, V. Mosch
OVERLEAF: Entrance to the Musical Theatre with Debis headquarters in the background. Photograph, V. Mosch

Potsdamer Platz, Berlin

Tjibaou Cultural Centre
Nouméa, New Caledonia

ABOVE: Concept sketch
BELOW: Panoramic view. Photograph, J. Gollings
OPPOSITE LEFT: Aerial view. Photograph, W. Wassal
OPPOSITE MIDDLE: Photograph, J. Gollings
OPPOSITE RIGHT: Photograph, W. Wassal

The Tjibaou Cultural Centre is not a monumental building, which would have been inappropriate in the Pacific, but a group of villages with their own pathways and public spaces. The first comprises a permanent exhibition of Kanak culture, space for temporary exhibitions, an auditorium, and an amphitheatre for open-air performances. The second contains a multimedia library and offices for the centre's historians and researchers. The third houses the administrative services; one of its constructions is a debating room, another a school room.

In this project, Piano, with the close cooperation of an anthropoligist, has created a modern language that expresses the traditions of Kanak culture. It is at one with the geography of the island and succeeds in creating the tension that will bind it to the life of its inhabitants.

C O S M

*"Voluptuous and
sexy through and through"*

(Flash Art)

**Ernesto Neto, who was born in Rio de Janeiro, creates sensuous sculptural worlds that you can enter and experience.
Uncanny and beautiful, Neto's environments are places for discovery and dreaming, wonder and contemplation.
His dominant material is a flexible, milky white lycra fabric that he stretches and shapes into sensual, sheer environments
and elegantly poised individual forms. Some of these are womb-like, with abject pink orifices along the inner walls.
Others hang as pendulums, like magical pods on the verge of explosion, using gravity to create the structural tension of
the piece. Neto positions and grounds these cloths with weighted pockets filled with sand and spices, that fill the
installations with their aromas and the gallery with stimulating smells.**

From an exhibition of newly commissioned works at the ICA, London.

rama

An irreverent selection of
international news, views,
projects and buildings,
exhibitions and recent
events worldwide.

[PROCAR UNIVERSE - PRAMA VISIONS]

O P R A M A

An exhibition at the Art Institute of Chicago:
Rebirth of Bilbao – Guggenheim Museum and beyond

Bilbao, the capital of Bizkaia (Biscay), which is located in the Basque region of northern Spain, is currently undergoing a remarkable cultural and economic renewal, tied in large part to a major government-sponsored building and infrastructure improvement thrust. A substantial decline in the ancient city's industrial and economic base in the 1970s and 80s forced the city to essentially reinvent itself – with the most famous result so far being architect Frank Gehry's Guggenheim Museum.

An imaginative exhibition design by Spanish architect Xavier Vendrell is the background for a broad range of drawings, plans, models, and photographs of the new projects.

While it is not unusual to see modern cities undertaking government-supported programmes to revitalise themselves, these programmes often receive impetus from specific events, such as a world fair or the Olympic games. In the case of Bilbao, however, no single happening can be identified

the transformation of a city

Bilbao

projects and architects

Abando Intermodal Passenger Station
James Stirling and Michael Wilford

Abandoibarra Riverfront Development Master Plan
Cesar Pelli, Balmori & Associates, Eugenio Aguinaga y Asociados

Abandoibarra Pedestrian Bridge
Lorenzo Fernández Ordóñez and Ignacio Bartolomé Biot

Abandoibarra Retail and Leisure Complex
Robert A.M. Stern

Riverfront Park, Abandoibarra
Javier Lopez Chollet and Marta Dalmau

Bilbao Metro
Foster and Partners

Euskalduna Performing Arts and Conference Centre
Federico Soriano and Dolores Palacios

Eusko Tram, Bilbao Tram System,
Ingenieria IDOM-Semaly

Fine Arts Museum of Bilbao Addition,
Luis M. Uriarte

Guggenheim Museum Bilbao,
Frank O. Gehry

Enlargement of the Port of Bilbao, Phase 3,
Manuel Santos, Jesús Villanueva, Javier Uzcanga, José Ma. Pico, Fernando Revuelta, Engineers

Sondika Airport Terminal and Control Tower,
Santiago Calatrava

Uribitarte High-Rise Housing,
Arata Isozaki

Master Plan for Water Purification,
Consorcio de Aguas Bilbao Bizkaia

University Pumping Station,
Javier and Valentín Galdos Tobalina

Zubi Zuri Pedestrian Bridge,
Santiago Calatrava

as the catalyst behind the initiatives that are taking place in the city. Rather, a combination of economic and political realities – the decline of traditional heavy industry, an expanding demand for modern urban services, and the increased responsibilities of local and regional governments – along with creative approaches to strategic planning, gave rise to a series of developments in a relatively short period of time. As Bilbao looks back to its origins and celebrates its 700th anniversary, it also looks forward to a future that is, in essence, being defined by these architectural and infrastructure projects. The Guggenheim, already generally considered to be one of the great buildings of the twentieth century, has garnered international attention for the Basque city since it opened in 1976, but other significant projects have also been taking shape.

The Bilbao Metro, a completely new underground system designed by Foster began operation in 1995 after many years of planning. A national architectural competition has resulted in a new Performing Arts and Conference Centre which provides space for concerts, operas, and professional meetings. The shipping port, historically a key component of the region's economy, has been moved and expanded; and an airport designed by Santiago Calatrava is under construction.

They illustrate how one city has tackled some unique challenges and created a new vision for the future, granting architecture a major role in redefining the city.

OPPOSITE: Aerial photograph of Bilbao
BELOW AND INSETS: Guggenheim Museum Bilbao
Photographs, AP-NA

505 UNION STATION:
Section at NORTH WINDOW WALL

SECTION - A

An 11-storey, 300,000 sq.ft building close to the International District of Seattle

THE SPACE NEEDLE, A WINDOW TO THE NORTHWEST, FRAMED BY THE 2nd AVENUE
CORRIDOR, CARVING OUT NORTH WALL AS A WINDOW BACK TO SEATTLE.

PLAN: FLOOR 10

Paul Allen and Jody Paton of Vulcan Northwest required a building of international importance and design that at the same time will be of great pride to the people of Seattle.

505 Union Station respects the site and its neighbouring buildings while its innovative design gives a new identity to the area. The design creates a powerful dialogue between historical Union Station and this contemporary building.

Daniel Libeskind
Jewish Museum San Francisco

L'Chaim: To Life

The design for The Jewish Museum San Francisco (JMSF) provides a place for activities, and a symbol dedicated to the revitalisation of Jewish life in San Francisco and beyond.

Such a building, rooted in the Jewish imagination and opening itself to the diverse contemporary currents of life, will be a fundamental contribution to the renaissance of Yerba Buena Center.

The challenge, significance, and potential of this site and the programme of The Jewish Museum San Francisco are themselves part of the cultural process symbolising the foundation of a new and innovative Jewish institution in San Francisco – an institution that will deal with continuity and identity. This relationship is revealed by the struggle to make space in this delicate location.

The site of the JMSF is an abandoned Power Substation designed by Willis Polk at the turn of the twentieth century. The building of the Museum will provide access to new spaces for new programmes through the simple yet elegant Polk Facade of the Power Substation. The new spaces will be incorporated within the old structure and will articulate a close relationship to the new Four Seasons Hotel and the pedestrian connector.

The atmosphere of the old Power Substation is carefully retained, while at the same time providing entirely new programmes and circulation spaces for The Jewish Museum San Francisco. The visitor is made aware of the old parameters of the Power Substation: the walls where batteries and equipment were once lodged, as well as the skylights and the restored south facade. In contrast and to complement this experience of history, the visitor will also experience the reconfigured spatial form of the new extension. History does not come to an end but opens to the future; history is a dynamic ground.

The site, a complex urban locus, provides the necessary pressure for the emergence of a unique form and energy. The Jewish Museum San Francisco will make visible the relationship between the new and the old, tradition and innovation, celebrating the City's past and reinvigorating it for the future. It will transform the physical energy associated with the legacy of the Power Substation to the power of human communication and imagination. Though small in comparison to the context of the neighbourhood, the building will become a metal-clad jewel like a beacon glowing for the future.

The JMSF building is based on the Hebrew word *l'chaim*, which means "to life." The two

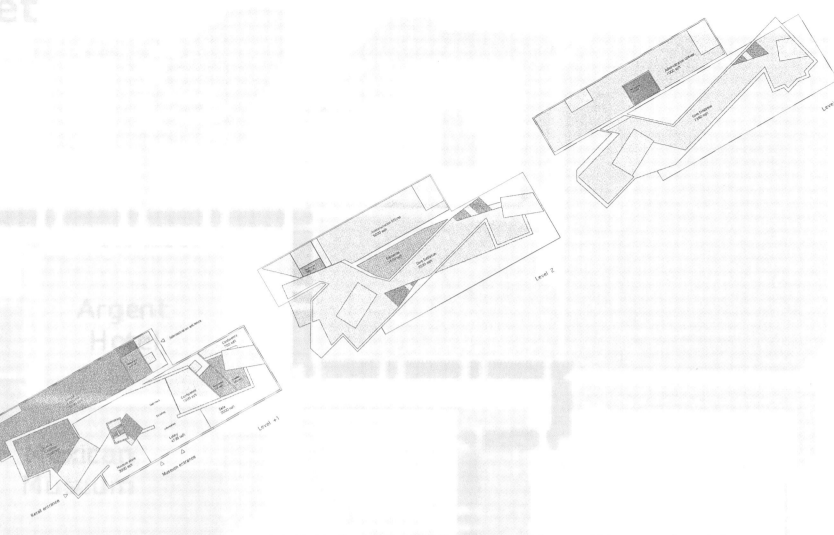

BACKGROUND: Jewish
Museum San Francisco,
site plan
OPPOSITE AND ABOVE:
Plans. (From left to right)
level -1, level +1, level +2,
level +3

Hebrew letters of *chai* (with all their symbolic, mathematical and emblematic structure) are literally the life source and the form of the Museum. In the Jewish tradition, letters are not mere signs but are substantial participants in the story they create. Thus, the spatiality of *chai* – a fundamental emblem of Jewish life – will be experienced as a full dynamic movement responding to the many levels of interpretation this word possesses.

The building brings together the activities of the Museum, the fullness of the senses and emotions by weaving the themes of exhibition, education, and knowledge for both Jews and non-Jews alike. It is the celebration of Jewish imagination and unity within the context of an evolving and developing history.

The new building is based on the unprecedented spaces created by the two letters of the *chai*: the *chet*, which provides an overall continuity for the core exhibition, and the yud, located on the pedestrian connector, which gives a new identity to the Power Substation. Together, these letters and their meaning constitute a special emblem for the ongoing development of the Yerba Buena Center, a symbol of the importance of culture, art, history and people to a civilised society.

The Jewish experience presented in this discourse of forms will engage both the Jewish and non-Jewish public with the image of a newly emerging Jewish-American identity. It will deal with the issues of imagination, creativity, vitality, and access.

The spaces and their programmes will delve into the depths of the Jewish spirit and celebrate the discovery and relevance of Jewish culture for all.

Visitors enter through the old, grandiose entrance of the Power Substation. The entire ground-level lobby, with its café and shop, reveals a dramatic view of the Power Substation skylights and the *chai*. The multipurpose theatre, temporary exhibitions, and educational services and administration spaces are integrated throughout the scheme.

Just as the fundamental concept of The Jewish Museum San Francisco is *L'chaim* – "*To Life,*" so does the building seek to contribute a powerful new structure, traversing the Power Substation, to the exciting Yerba Buena Center development. The discovery of the richness of Jewish culture will become an enduring magnet, offering the public the opportunity to share a universal heritage.

Daniel Libeskind

tomas taveira
Olaias Expo Metro Station

Tomas Taveira was largely responsible for the development of the residential area of Olaias in Lisbon which he completed some 20 years ago. He now returns to the area to build the $46 million metro station on the prestigious Expo line, for which he has designed all the elements – including the metal ceilings and support details – and the highly colourful spaces.

The official opening of the Museum is scheduled for 2001 and yet such has been the success of the building based on its architecture alone – over 160,000 people have already visited it to view the work of Daniel Libeskind – that the Director felt it necessary to explain that visitors do not come for the spectacular architecture alone. Despite the optimism surrounding the installation of the planned permanent exhibition, there is a strong voice that the qualities of the space itself be recognised and that it be left empty. But Tom L. Freudenheim, the Deputy Director, points out that the building was never designed just to have paintings on the walls but to provide a place to explicate history and culture. He expects the spaces to work well with the narrative exhibition now being developed.

"To be housed in Daniel Libeskind's world famous building is a real stroke of luck for our museum. Next to Germany's parliament building, the Reichstag, it each month. More than 160,000 people from Germany and abroad have passed through our halls. It is of major national and even international importance that

jewish m

Photograph, AP-NA

dered the leading architectural attraction in the new capital. Although the building is still empty, thousands come to join guided tours awn of the 21st century, the largest Jewish Museum in Europe is being built in the heart of Germany." W. Michael Blumenthal, Director

museum

berlin

berlin

regenerating meaning

I cannot deny that in pursuing the elimination of meaning I had in mind the attainment of freedom or liberation from oppression of a preestablished character, but freedom or liberation was, I believe, also the main theme of the Modernist Movement. Freedom or liberation does not mean random, wholesale destruction but is, I believe, the basic premise of human existence. Destruction that is not based on such a premise can only produce a wasteland. The question we confront today is how to create and shape human existence in a state of liberation and freedom.

Hiromi Fujii

Incompleteness as a theme

Hiromi Fujii

Today we can see a wide variety of architectural styles. There are buildings in eclectic styles that seem to carry on the post-modern movement, traditional buildings that express a consciousness of past history, buildings that project contemporary high-tech or machine images, and recently buildings that are deconstructionist or chaotic.

ABOVE: Ushimado International Art Festival Centre, axonometric drawing
PREVIOUS PAGES: Marchi Project

Very few of these buildings possess a single, integrated style. More often, they are mosaics of allusive images, fragments of images generated by private experience, or simulated images. For architecture this is indeed an age of images.

This is quite different from the situation in the 1960s, when there was, as a result of general adherence to doctrine, only one goal and one direction.

The present situation may be accounted for by a variety of factors. I believe one of those factors is a change in people's awareness of consciousness.

Today there are very few people who still truly believe in past ideas of classicist architecture or in ideologically based explanations of architecture and who value only such ideas or explanations. By no means does our awareness of consciousness have a single origin. In the East as in the West, human conscious-ness is created out of a mosaic of traces of diverse cultural and historical encounters. Moreover, we do not all share the same consciousness; instead, our consciousness in large part has a private, individual dimension.

Given the multicentric and diverse nature of human consciousness or awareness, I believe it is anachronistic to think that the goal of design can be reduced, as it was in the past, to any single idea or ideology and that messages or meanings can be transmitted by organising and integrating everything around that idea or ideology. For an architect to strive toward such an objective is, I believe, pointless and futile.

In our present spiritual condition, the important question we architects must confront becomes, not what architectural theme we should adopt, but how diverse images and meanings may be generated.

In other words, what is important for architecture today is not "what" but "how," namely how meanings and images might be generated. When "what" used to be the goal of architecture, the reaching of that goal ended in completion. By comparison, when the issue is "how," there is no end, and only the process is apparent.

Since there is only process, architecture remains incomplete. Moreover, since architecture itself carries no meanings or message, it becomes something provisional and without presence.

Recognising the diversity of consciousness today, I am attempting to create a provisional, incomplete architecture that will make possible the generation of meaning. My efforts began some time ago. I began my design activities in 1970 and from the start I was interested in the anonymity of architecture and an open architectural aesthetic. My interest was not in an architecture that conveyed meaning or messages but in an architecture that could generate meanings.

The question we confront today is how to create and shape human existence in a state of liberation and freedom.

The generation of meaning and the creation of place are my attempt to provide an answer to that question.
Hiromi Fujii
from a lecture given at Rice Univercity

The theme of the 7th International Venice Architecture Biennale as defined by its director, Rome-based architect Massimiliano Fuksas, is "Cities: less aesthetics, more ethics," to which he devotes the major international exhibition. According to Fuksas it "aims to pick up the thread that was broken at the end of the seventies. The great heritage of research, ideas and utopias produced by the sixties..."

The British Pavilion is devoted to the work of four architects: Will Alsop, Nigel Coates, David Chipperfield and Zaha Hadid who all introduce a new grammar into the language of architecture – personal, poetic, irreverent and full of surprises. The exhibition shows how inspirational architecture can transform not only the urban landscape but also the lives of those who inhabit it.

Alsop & Störmer's new building for C/Plex, ART in the Community in West Bromwich is destined, with its public square, to become the focus of the town. It is programmed with electronic images and light, a place for dance, performance, and celebration.

David Chipperfield Architects' large-scale models demonstrate the volumetric, spatial and material concerns of their buildings.

Nigel Coates and Doug Branson fold many of their recent projects – both built and conceptual – into an imaginary landscape, with other expressive media, monuments and buildings to create a vision of Ecstacity, a continuously evolving hypothesis for city planning.

Zaha Hadid presents a series of recent projects that work with ribbons. Three of them are bridges, funnelling and distributing various trajectories; the fourth moves

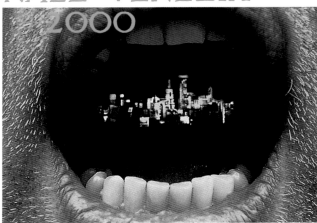

GRAN BRETAGNA BIENNALE DI VENEZIA 2000

Branson Coates, Ecstacity

visitors through the story of the Mind. This selection on the basis of a set of related analogical themes – flexing and folding ribbons as well as splintering bundles – is a reflection of how Hadid develops work via families of conceptually related projects.

In addition the new National Assembly for Wales by The Richard Rogers Partnership to be constructed in Cardiff Bay forms part of the international exhibition.

The Venice Biennale will be featured extensively in the next issue of NEW ARCHITECTURE.

Pompidou Centre

Elysian Fields

The recent exhibition at the Pompidou Centre was organised by the magazine Purple, created in 1992 by Elein Fleiss and Olivier Zahm. The Purple Institute presents poetic, dreamlike spaces bordering on abstraction, by forty artists of all ages and disciplines, that constitute an alternative to the commercialised, mass produced dreams of today.

Tate Modern, Bankside

Tate Director:
Sir Nicholas Serota

Tate Modern Director:
Lars Nittve

Architects:
Herzog & de Meuron

Building Facts

Total Project Costs:
£134.5 million
Under £2,000 per sq.m

Total internal floor area:
34,000 sq.m

Total display space:
4,000 sq.m

Chimney height:
325 ft (St Paul's 375 ft)

Number of bricks:
Approximately 4.2 million

New steel work:
3,750 tons

New timber floor:
Approximately 12,000 sq.m

New Turbine Hall roof:
524 glass panes

Length of new cabling:
218 miles

We have used a kind of 'Aikido' strategy: you employ your opponent's energy for your own purposes. Instead of fighting it, you take the energy and shape it. *Jacques Herzog*

The best of international art, the best of 20th century art; that's what the Tate Modern is all about. *Sir Nicholas Serota*

For those of us familiar with the work of Herzog and de Meuron, we would expect an architectural statement and immaculate presentation of minimalist spaces and that is exactly what we found.

There is no doubt, however, that the one memorable space is the old turbine hall with its palette of black, grey and opaque glass. Whether it should be attributed to Herzog and de Meuron, to Sir Giles Gilbert Scott, or to the requirements of an earlier industrial age is almost irrelevant. The effect is breathtaking. As for the rest, there is the little matter of over 80 galleries on the upper floors and one of the greatest collections of modern art in the world. The architects have provided a description of the building to accompany their own opening exhibition. We present here an edited version in words and images.

PREVIOUS PAGES: Chimney and Tate Modern facade during the light show at the official opening, May 11, 2000
Photograph, AP-NA
BACKGROUND: Reception area to the galleries on level 5
Photograph, Grant Smith
ABOVE LEFT: General view from Southwark bridge
Photograph, Tate Modern
ABOVE MIDDLE: The Turbine Hall (level 1) with the Towers by Louise Bourgeois and the floating bay windows on level 3
Photograph, Grant Smith
ABOVE RIGHT: Gallery room, level 5, with window overlooking lower levels.
Photograph, AP-NA
OPPOSITE LEFT: The restaurant, up into the light beam on level 7, with a view over the Thames and Saint Paul's Cathedral
Photograph, Grant Smith
OPPOSITE RIGHT: The Platform, level 2, with the giant spider by Louise Bourgeois.
Photograph, AP-NA

Base Camp, Level 2

The exhibition examines the subtle ways in which the architects have managed to adapt and celebrate Gilbert Scott's massive industrial structure. At the base camp, a large model along with a film and statement by the architects introduce the project. The rest of the exhibition takes the form of a stroll in and around Tate Modern.

The Ramp, Level 1

The ramp is one of the main ways into the gallery and one of the most significant architectural interventions. Outside, the ground dips towards the entrance, becoming the enormous concrete ramp, which then leads down to the turbine hall floor (situated below the level of the Thames). As the ramp passes through the low entrance the sense of compression followed by

sudden release, as the hall is revealed, makes the space seem all the more vast. The turbine hall run like a street through the entire length and height of the building. The new glass facade of the gallery rises to the north, its layout visible at a single glance: entrance, shop, educational facilities, auditorium, concourses and exhibition spaces.

Hidden Spaces, Level 1

This window looks through to the area below the switch-house. The switch-house continues to be operated by London Electricity as a supply station. Beyond is the dramatic space consisting of cylindrical rooms, arranged like a three-leaf clover, that once housed the oil tanks that fuelled the power station turbines. In a later phase, it is proposed

that these rooms, and the floors above them, will be opened up to make them accessible from the garden to the south. They could house a library, or more exhibition spaces.

The Turbine Hall, Level 2

From the platform, visitors can look out over the vast space of the turbine hall. It is intended as a public space, like a plaza, open to everyone, whether they have come to look at installations created by artists especially for the hall, to see an exhibition in the galleries, or are simply passing through. The facade of the gallery rises on the north side of the turbine hall. This area was once an openwork steel frame where the many boilers and other machinery that ran the power station were installed. Seven new floors have replaced this steel frame. The elongated glass bodies of light in the facade are the bay windows, which offer a glimpse of the galleries beyond. They break up the vertical steel supports of the facade, and make a visual connection with the light beam on top of the building.

The Platform, Level 2

The platform is the last remaining evidence of a floor that once stretched

the entire length of the turbine hall. By removing the floor we have revealed the extraordinary scale and dimensions of Gilbert Scott's power station. The platform acts as a bridge between the entrance and galleries to the north and the switch-house to the south. It was conceived not only as a link between two wings of the building, but also as a way of connecting Tate Modern to its surround environment. The river walk along the Thames runs straight up to the north entrance and into the centre of the gallery. Once the next phase of development has been completed, visitors will be able to walk on across the platform to the south, continuing through the switch-house area, through a southern entrance into the new gardens, and then to the city beyond.

The Bay Windows, Level 3

The bay windows are self-contained spaces, which are more intimately proportioned than the adjacent concourses and galleries. They are convenient meeting points, places to pause and rest. They also offer spectacular, vertiginous viewpoints onto the turbine hall below. Seen from the turbine hall they look like floating bodies of light, part of the same architectural family as the light beam on top of the building.

The Galleries, Level 3

Some museums and galleries are divided into a series of hierarchical exhibition spaces - a floor of large, height rooms for monumental works, and a separate level of smaller spaces for works such as photographs or drawings. At Tate Modern, there are three floors of exhibition spaces, all equal in importance. Each of the three floors contains rooms of differing propor-

tions. As certain points walls can also be added or removed, allowing the dimensions to be tailored to the precise requirements of a particular installation. The spaces are all at least 5m high and some are significantly higher, like the top-lit galleries on level five, and, in the double-height gallery, which rises to 12m (the dimensions of the power station windows which have been retained). This dramatic vertical height

allows exciting opportunities for the display of large-scale works. There are no connecting joints between walls and floors, or floors and ceilings. The oak floors are untreated which lends the spaces a raw sensuality, while the dark, smooth concrete floor on level five makes an unexpected contrast with the works of art, especially those of classical modernism.

The Chimney, Level 4

In the next phase of Tate Modern's development it is proposed that the chimney be converted into an observation tower. Two staircases and two lifts will take visitors up to a height of 93m for breathtaking views over London.

The Stairway, Level 5

The stairway connects all seven storeys of the gallery and functionally

complements the other two vertical support systems, the lifts and the escalator. The heavy steel construction with its flush wooden handrail, it s continuous band of light and its distinctively compact proportions represents an independent piece of architecture. The height of the stairs and the position of the landings influence the speed and rhythm at which we pass between the storeys. The balcony-like landings

also offer surprising viewpoints and spatial impressions.

The Clear Storey, Level 6

The view into the clear storey offers a backstage glimpse of the lighting facilities for Level 5. The clear storey is part of the light beam, which sits on top of the power station. It allows natural light to filter through the glass panels to the galleries below, and also provides artificial illumination, which is designed to mimic daylight as closely as possible. Lighting plays a significant role in the way we perceive a work of art. The light at Tate Modern is slightly different in every room, alternating between daylight, artificial light, and a mixture of both. Conservation and the different needs of particular works of art call for a maximum

precision in lighting control. For this reason, the glazing in the clear storey has to be translucent to prevent direct sunlight and shadows, but without unduly reducing or distorting the colour of the daylight. Two seats of blinds have been installed between the panes of glass, one to adjust the intensity of the light, and the other to block out light all together for times when the galleries need to be darkened.

The Light Beam, Level 7

From the very beginning, we entertained the idea of a huge body of light hovering above the heavy brick structure of the former power station. This body of light was to pour daylight into the galleries on he top floor, and at night, the direction of the artificial illumination would be reversed and would magically shine into the London skies.

The light beam proved to be a key concept in the development of many elements of Tate Modern's architecture. Seen from the outside, the horizontal shape of the light beam forms a distinctive counterpoint to the vertical thrust of the brick chimney - which was itself intended by Gilbert Scott as a response to the dome of St. Paul's, just across the river.

RIGHT: Night view of the exterior with light pouring out of the light beam
Photograph, Tate Modern
OPPOSITE: The ramp, level 1, leading to the Turbine Hall
Photograph, Grant Smith

The art of being modern in 84 galleries,

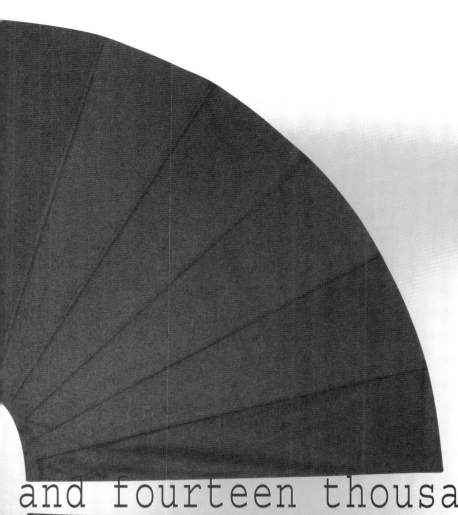

and fourteen thousand square metres

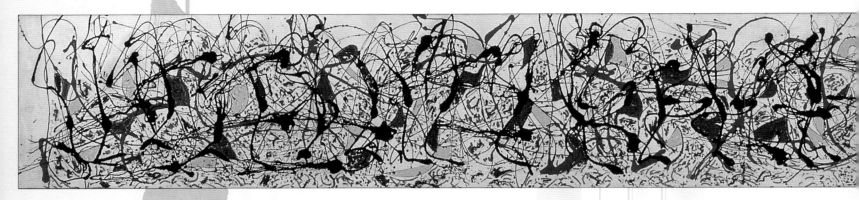

The displays are divided into four themed groups. Each theme occupies one suite of galleries and focuses on one of the major traditional categories of art, tracing some of the ways it has both continued and been transformed through the 20th century.

History/Memory/Society: The Grid

(OPPOSITE INSET:)
Carl Andre,
Equivalent VIII, 1966
fiberbricks, 12.7x68.6x229.2 cm

Sol Lewitt,
A Wall Divided Vertically into Fifteen Equal Parts, Each with a Different Line Direction and Colour, and All Combinations, 1970

Agnes Martin, *Morning*, 1965
Photograph, Mark Heathcote

Landscape/Matter/Environment

(ABOVE:)
Jackson Pollock,
Summertime: Number 9a, 1948
Oil, enamel and house paint on canvas
84.8x555 cm
BACKGROUND:
Joseph Beuys,
The End of the Twentieth Century, 1983-85
Basalt, clay and felt
Photograph, Grant Smith

Still Life/Object/Real Life

(RIGHT:)
Claes Oldenburg,
Soft Drainpipe – Blue (Cool) Version, 1967
Acrylic on canvas and steel
259.1x187.6x35.6 cm
Photograph, Tate Modern

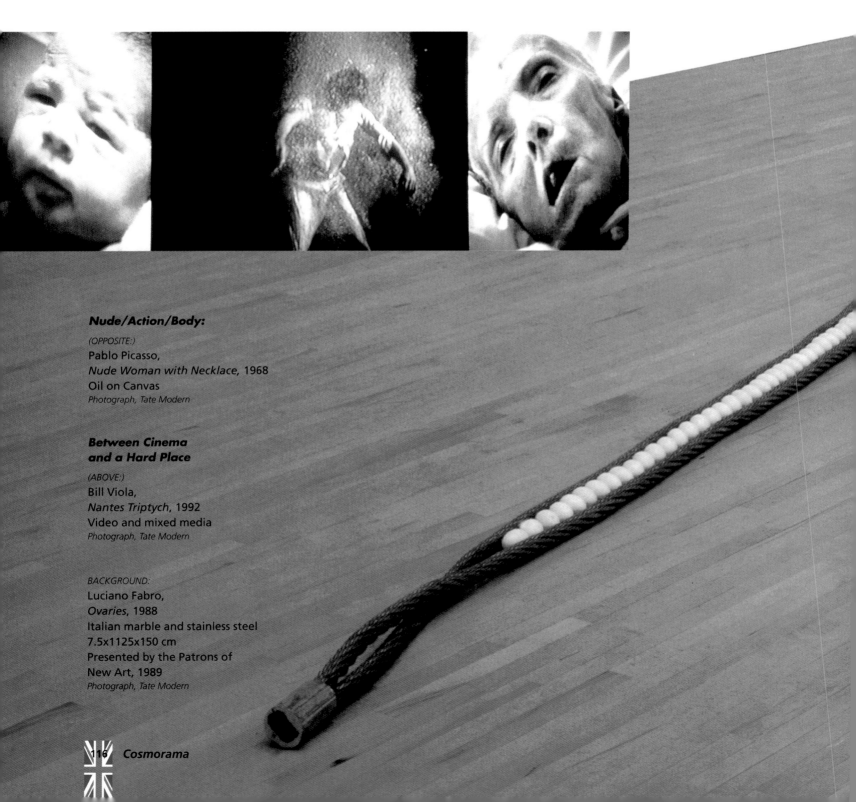

Between Cinema and a Hard Place , a temporary exhibition at Tate Modern, takes its title from a video work by the American artist Gary Hill, in which he explores the relationship between cinematic and real space. As well as films and videos, which investigate space through the immaterial play of light and sound, the exhibition includes works in which objects have a strong material presence. Many take the form of carefully staged environments demonstrating the radical switch that artists have made from presenting a window onto the world, to presenting a world in itself.

Nude/Action/Body:

(OPPOSITE:)
Pablo Picasso,
Nude Woman with Necklace, 1968
Oil on Canvas
Photograph, Tate Modern

**Between Cinema
and a Hard Place**

(ABOVE:)
Bill Viola,
Nantes Triptych, 1992
Video and mixed media
Photograph, Tate Modern

BACKGROUND:
Luciano Fabro,
Ovaries, 1988
Italian marble and stainless steel
7.5x1125x150 cm
Presented by the Patrons of
New Art, 1989
Photograph, Tate Modern

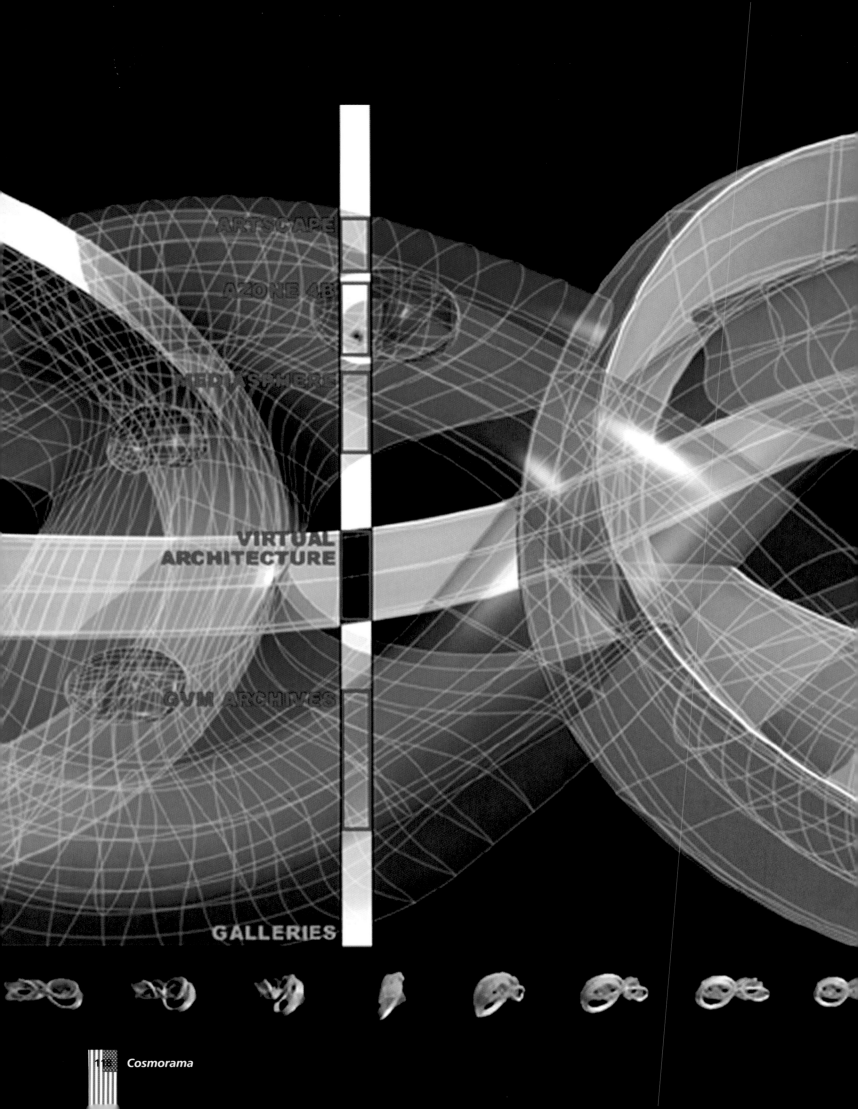

ARTSCAPE

A-ZONE 48

MEDIASPHERE

VIRTUAL
ARCHITECTURE

GVM ARCHIVES

GALLERIES

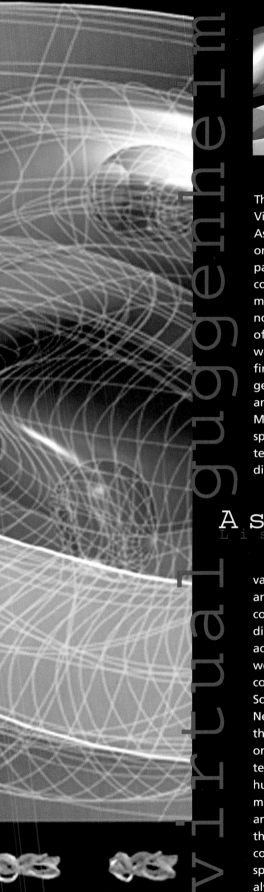

The first phase of the Guggenheim Virtual Museum, designed by Asymptote, has been launched on-line New Years Eve 2000 as part of a three-year initiative to construct an entirely new museum facility. The GVM will not only house and connect all of the Guggenheim Museums worldwide but will also be the first museum to contain art generated exclusively within and for the Internet. The Museum will contain ongoing special exhibits, a digital architecture archive as well as three-dimensional spaces linking the

form and permanence will without doubt persevere and another virtual architecture surfacing now in the digital domain of the Internet. Buildings, institutions, objects and space are now being constructed, navigated, experienced, comprehended and altered in their virtual states by countless people across the globe. This is a new architecture of liquidity, flux and mutability predicated on technological advances and fueled by a basic human need to probe the unknown. The path that both these architec-

and its valued pedagogical and cultural dimension all serve to form a unique scaffolding for the museum of the future. The Guggenheim Virtual Museum will emerge as an impressive and new architectural work by fusing information space, art, commerce and architecture. The resulting virtual architecture will be accessible from anywhere in the world, while uniting all the Guggenheim museums it will also be the first important virtual building to emerge in the twenty-first century.

Asymptote Architecture
Lise Anne Couture & Hani Rashid

various 'first reality' museums and amenities. The project will consist of navigable three-dimensional spatial entities accessible on the Internet as well as a 'real time' interactive component installed at the Soho Guggenheim location in New York City. For Asymptote this project brings forward their ongoing interest in merging technological possibilities with human experience and spatial manufacture.When speaking of an architecture for the future there are two conditions to consider. Primarily the physical space of architecture as we have always known it, enclosure,

tures, the real and the virtual, will inevitably take will be one of convergence and merging. Historically architecture has always struggled with this dialectic of the real and the virtual, at once architectures stability and actuality has always been tempered and by the metaphysical and the poetic. Today global networks and digital tools are the critical means by which architects navigate this trajectory into the future. The Guggenheim Virtual Museum originates and surfaces from such a state, where the museum's colorful past, its and historic architectural avant-garde

Hani Rashid along with Gregg Lynn lead a studio programme and exhibition at the U.S. Pavilion for the Seventh Venice Architecture Biennale, from June 18 to October 29. The programme features the work of architecture students from UCLA and Columbia and transforms the U.S. Pavilion into a research laboratory designed to investigate, produce and present a broad scope of new architectural schemes.

The central theme of the studio programme is new technology and its application to contemorary housing and other building archetypes.

As Max Hollein, U.S. Commissioner to the Venice Architecture Biennale, stated: "The state of our urban situation cannot be addressed solely with regard to its infrastructure and physical orientation".

Visible invisible

You cannot see the wind.

You can feel its breath on your skin but you cannot see it.

It is only the swaying of the trees that betrays its presence.

Tree branches are a device for visualising the wind.

FIBER WAVE is an artificial branch.

Trees are supple and pliant.

They yield softly, letting the wind pass through. They do not fight the wind.

They do not fight but are never defeated. When the wind dies down they regain their original shape.

This is not so with things people make. They are always fighting.

Buildings, bridges and towers.

They stand up against the wind, hard, strong and manly.

And sometimes they collapse.

FIBER WAVE is different. It does not fight. It is much like the trees. It is an artificial plant that changes its shape to relate to the wind.

The wind determines its shape. It is a design-less design.

And **FIBER WAVE II** is like light as well.

A trembling, rustling light.

It is not the wind of this place that causes the light to tremble.

It is a wind that can only be blowing in another world.

Across the ocean, in a far desert, or a sweltering city.

On green planets, red stars, frozen methane seas.

Somewhere on the Net.

That wind is visible. Right now, right here.

Technology, living things, the Net.

All fusing together.

The touch of liquids melting the city.

FIBER WAVE III is the virtual development version.

Through the Net it responds to the wind of a virtual world.

FIBER WAVE III makes the invisible wind to be visible.

To make the invisible thing in the world to be visible: That is the mission of architecture and the role of art.

Design-less Design

FIBER WAVE rods swaying in the wind like a field of grass. Its movements are protean and at the same time harmonious. They are not however specified by the designer. Only the flexibility of the rods in response to the force of the wind and the arrangement of the rods determine how it will move.

The "form" of motion is not designed.

All that was designed is the "code" defining its physical properties and arrangement. Yet even though its form and movement are free and diverse, they are not random: one senses the underlying regularities of natural law. The method used here is not one of directly specifying the form, that which appears on the surface, but rather of deciding the mechanism which gives birth to form as its effect.

Such a method suggests new possibilities, which may open onto the future of "design".

fiber wave DIGITAL

Makoto Sei Watanabe

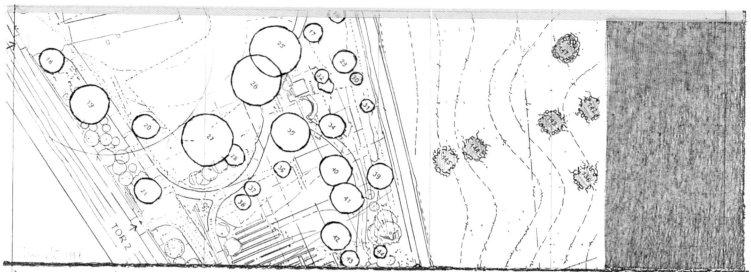

Wrapped Trees (Project for Fondation Beyeler and Berower Park, Riehen, Switzerland) Baselstrasse, Bachtelenweg, Muhleteich

wrapped trees

Fondation Beyeler and Berower Park, Riehen, Switzerland

Christo and Jeanne-Claude

The trees are located in the park around the Fondation Beyeler and in the adjacent meadow as well as along the creek of Berower Park. In total 178 trees were wrapped with 55,000 sq.m of the woven polyester fabric used every winter in Japan to protect the trees from frost and heavy snow, and 23.1km of rope.

The Berower park, which is located northeast of Basel on the German border, includes a great diversity of trees: chestnut, oak, ash, plum, cherry, linden, gingko, beech, birth, sycamore, maple, catalpa, hazelnut and golden weeping willow with heights varying from 2m to 25 m and diameters from 1m to 14.5m.

Before the leaves start gowing again the wrapping will be removed and the materials will be recycled.

Christo and Jeanne-Claude have worked with trees for many years and the "Wrapped Trees" in Riehen are the outcome of thirty-two years of effort.

The branches of the trees push the translucent fabric outwards, creating dynamic volumes of light and shadow that move in the wind with new forms and surfaces shaped by the ropes on the fabric.

OPPOSITE: Collage. In two parts: Pencil, charcoal, crayon, topographic map on tracing paper, fabric sample and tape. 30.5 x 77.5 cm and 70.5 x 77.5 cm
THIS PAGE: Drawing. Pencil, charcoal pastel and crayon. 165 x 106.6 cm
OVERLEAF: Wrapped Trees, Berower Park. Photographs, Wolfgang Volz

The BA Bienal, a unique major international architectural achievement was founded and is still administered by Jorge Glusberg, a wealthy industrialist, patron of architecture and the arts, and director of the National Museum of Fine Arts of Argentina. It is Glusberg's personality and contacts that facilitate the success of the highly ambitious programme of carefully balanced speakers chosen internationally and participants ranging from the well established to very new voices and faces. Here, we present a brief overview of the Bienal in a selection of images and text from the presentations and supporting range of exhibitions. Various lectures and projects are featured more extensively elsewhere in this volume.

P I C T O R I A L   S U R V E Y

Massimiliano Fuksas
Peace Centre

A home port for all sailors and a haven for the shipwrecked...
Peace is a spiritual condition, an aspiration: tension and utopia. This project represents the venue of an encounter, a debate, reasoning and solutions...
Peace cannot be enclosed in wrapping: it is, rather, a sensation of fullness and serenity that can be communicated through a place, or through architecture. I have thought of a series of layers, a building that represents TIME and PATIENCE in strata of alternating materials representing places that have suffered heavily...
The basement becomes a large plaza, an empty space dissected lengthwise by two symmetrical ramps leading inside. This dark and low-ceilinged area leads to the inside of the well of light that is open for the whole height of the building, where the reception area is situated. MF

OPPOSITE: Peace Centre, Model. Photograph, Studio Fuksas

introduced by Jorge Glusberg

McLuhan's "global village" may have become a reality, but nothing can ever take the place of direct contact between the people who live in that village.

In fact, person-to-person communication is stimulated and expanded by the communications satellites and aircraft, which largely make this global experience possible.

Since 1985 the Buenos Aires Bienal has been one of these new communication forums, facilitating encounters and exchanges among architects from all over the world. For one week, part of the "global village" comes to Buenos Aires. At the end of the week, we know more about architecture in the rest of the world, and the rest of the world knows more about our architecture. This is because we know more about the people who design and produce architecture, having heard them speak and viewed their work. In short, we have a greater knowledge of other people's lives and aspirations, for that is what architecture is all about. Man devised architecture to complete the process of his own development. The Socratic "know yourself" should also be applied to

the architecture in which that "self" lives, which is its immediate and natural extension.

In essential terms, architecture is all about meetings and exchanges: of all the arts and sciences, architecture alone endeavours to create the physical conditions in which people can meet and exchange ideas and experiences, whether this is done in the simplest house or the most complex airports, in the largest megalopolis or the tiniest town. The creation of the physical conditions for meetings and exchanges, which play a defining and formative role in human lives, is the first step towards self-realisation.

Some 2500 years ago, the early Greek philosophers understood intuitively that human beings are only fully human when they relate to other human beings. This insight has been developed and strengthened by theologians, poets, jurists and cultural theorists: the recognition of the other, this principle of "otherness" is the basis of laws, beliefs, political systems and aesthetic realities.

Architecture, then, is a byword for "otherness," for which it provides scope for action and verification. A

Bernardo Fort-Brescia

ABOVE LEFT: Performing Arts Centre,
Dijon, France. Interior.
ABOVE RIGHT: Performing Arts Centre,
Dijon. Exterior. Photographs, Paul Maurer.
TOP RIGHT: Festival Walk, Hong Kong.
Canyon. Photograph, Ralph Thomas.
All photographs, courtesy Arquitectonica.

Mario Lara

Apartment building, Barranco, Lima, Peru.

building, or a city, is the initial concrete expression of the recognition of the value of other people. Architecture lays the foundations for communication between people.

The Buenos Aires Bienal is nothing other than the externalisation of all these certainties and potentialities of architecture. Meetings and exchanges involving architects and architectural works are meetings and exchanges among thousands of people represented by these architects and architectural works. The Bienal is a vast, multidimensional expression of the principle of "otherness," offering scope for the development of fellowship on a world-wide scale.

The philosopher Gabriel Marcel wrote: "A powerful secret force assures me that if others did not exist, I would not exist either." It is no exaggeration to state that architecture imparts that "powerful secret force" to the reality of daily life, enables it to emanate from within man and ensures that it ceases being secret whilst remaining powerful.

Recognition of the Other implies living with other people; empathy and, consequently, appropriation are united in a paradigmatic and absolute way in archi-

Vittorio Gregotti

Siemens building, Birocca, Milan. Western façade, entrance hall and reception space.

Mario Botta

Library in Dortmund, Germany.
Photograph, Cornelia Suhan.

Berardo Dujovne

Puerto Madero development.

tectural objects. Man extends his being to build reality and makes it his own: it becomes part of him and is his living environment. However, within that built reality he relates to other people who are their own persons and have their own living environment. All people therefore can achieve full self-realisation through (and in) works of architecture.

Like its predecessors, the 7th Bienal aims to build, within Buenos Aires, a city consisting of buildings, streets and squares, designed by foreign and Argentine architects through lectures, exhibitions of their work, the discussion of ideas and matching of theories.

Neither the buildings, nor the streets, nor the squares of this city were demolished at the end of the previous Bienal. The products of those meetings and exchanges, which gave rise to the foundations and roofs, walls and windows, doors and floors, green areas and enclosed outdoor spaces, are still standing. They are the lasting, valuable outcome of that Bienal, making a positive contribution to human development and the attainment of a better world.

Jorge Glusberg

Paul Chemetov

Travel information 107.7 Radio Mast, France.
Programme: Construction of pylons and technical buildings for radio stations. The height of the mast is 54 metres. Six of them are scheduled to be built.

Abraham Zabludovsky

Multipurpose Auditorium and Convention Centre, Tuxtla Gutiérrez, Chiapas.

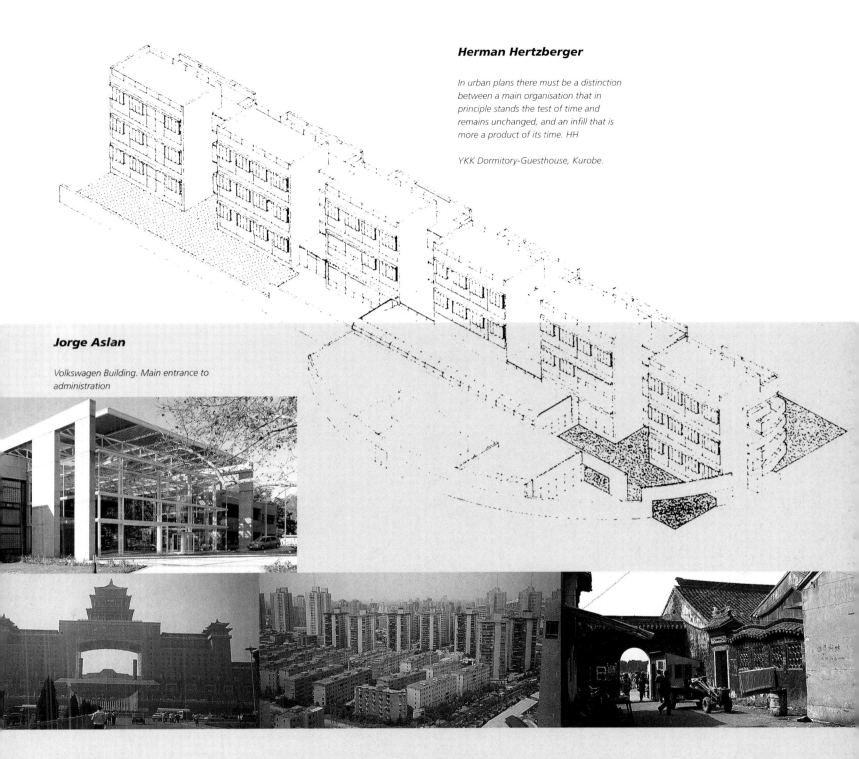

Herman Hertzberger

In urban plans there must be a distinction between a main organisation that in principle stands the test of time and remains unchanged, and an infill that is more a product of its time. HH

YKK Dormitory-Guesthouse, Kurobe.

Jorge Aslan

Volkswagen Building. Main entrance to administration

Zhang Qinnan   On the "Mutation in Chinese Cities"

...Many attempts to retain tradition have failed. The vulgarised way of adding traditional roofs to high rise towers was resisted by many architects from the outset. Serious attempts to renew and revitalise courtyard houses in Beijing and lane houses in Shanghai were resisted by most developers. I.M. Pei created a milestone in new Chinese architecture in the Fragrance Hill Hotel, which is highly successful from the architectural point of view but a failure financially because of its location and bad

management. And so tradition seems to be fighting a losing battle. A recent figure estimates that at the end of the twentieth century China had opened up a market totalling 700 billion US dollars in trade and investment, and so the future would seem to belong to generic cities and generic architecture.
But still I find hope in referring to history. From the early years of the twentieth century, there appeared a new type of urban living in the form of lane housing, which was a

combination of the row houses of Britain and Continental Europe and the clustered courtyard houses in the lower Yangtsze River towns... These lane houses differed in quality and cost, meeting the demands of indigenous middle-class Chinese residents in the city and they were highly profitable for developers. If the market could create an urban culture then, why not now? I have tried to introduce some community spirit into our planning but my attempts were rejected... I have experienced two types of international

style architecture: the neo-classicism of colonial architecture built in the early years of the 20th century; and the modernist international style of the mid 20th century. They were mainly one-way traffic from the developed to the undeveloped. And now that the earth is getting smaller and cross-cultural exchanges have become more popular, my hope is that a two-way traffic in transcultural architecture will create a third generation of international style. Life would then become more interesting than in generic cities.

Suha Ozkan
The Aga Khan Award for Architecture

The phenomenon of rural-to-urban migration that affected nearly all third world cities, beginning in the 1950s and continuing still today, greatly accelerated the transformation of environments in the Islamic world. Novel modes of building for urban survival became widespread, and squatter settlements and unlicensed or informal building added a harsh new reality to the rapid transformation of the fringes of cities, even as their historical cores were being destroyed from within.

Whose fault is it? The question remains permanently unanswered. Is it the Modern Movement in architecture which caused this degeneration, or is it "Modernity" itself, and the licensing of meaningless uniformity? Or, has it come about as the result of veiled forces in society that have pursued selfish or political short-term goals, and disguised their efforts in the name of "Modernity"? Since the late 1970s, these questions have been endlessly debated, and the debate will probably continue indefinitely. Is it because architects and architectural thinkers prefer to adopt strong, partisan attitudes instead of trying to understand the forces that brought about the situation?

Ricardo Legorreta

College of Santa Fe Visual Arts Centre, Santa Fe, New Mexico. Photograph, Lourdes Legorreta.

Richard Henriquez

Environmental Sciences Building, Trent University, Ontario, Canada. Central gathering space and ocular skylight.

Cesar Pelli

Petronas Towers, Kuala Lumpur, Malaysia

We tried to respond to the climate, to the dominant Islamic culture, and to the sense of form and patterning that I could perceive in traditional Malaysian buildings and objects. We also worked very hard to avoid any sense of a cultural pastiche. It is too easy to go overboard. Adapting a contemporary design to a place requires respect, control and considerable sensitivity...
The most important artistic decision was to make the towers figurative and symmetrically composed... The towers we designed are not only symmetrical but figurative, creating in addition a figurative space between them. This space is the key element in the composition. Each tower has its own vertical axis, but the axis of the total composition is in the centre of the void. CP

BELOW: Photograph Jeff Goldberg/Esto.
BACKGROUND: Aerial view. Photograph, J.Apicella/CP&A

Kiyonori Kikutake

MK Dom
(Techno Projects: Information Society's Nodal Point - Dome)

The individuality of the Techno Project will give people richer dreams, and it will be of great help in the acquisition and widening of a universality that will bring a better future and a more desirable environment. KK

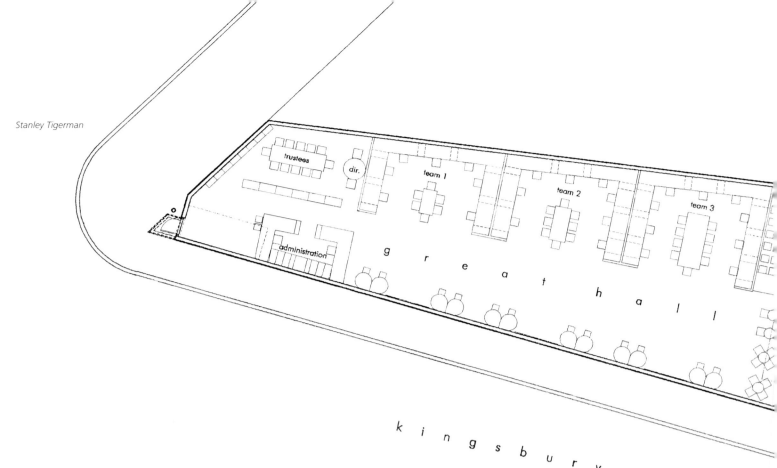

Stanley Tigerman

trustees

dir.

team 1

team 2

team 3

administration

g r e a t h a l l

k i n g s b u r y

Csaba Rosta

MADI Bridge, Györ, Hungary.

The MADI Bridge creates connections between different people and their culture and between the second and the third millennium.

Dominique Perrault

Bibliothèque de France, Paris.

Léon Krier

"It is obvious that, apart from a few exceptions, modernist buildings are as a rule not in keeping with historic city centres: the Palais-Royal, the Maison Carrée in Nîmes, the Louvre forecourt were not in need of their recent additions. We may well ask ourselves what has been enhanced by what... If these costly operations had been built in the suburbs, there would be scarcely a mention of them. But millions of visitors are used as evidence of the exceptional popularity of various ostentatious modernist monuments, whereas the popularity of Port-Grimaud and Williamsburg is denounced as politically dangerous. It may be absurd to force certain architects ot design traditional facades in historic centres; but surely it is even more absurd to pretend that without dramatic interventions historic centres lack vitality and dynamism."

Stanley Tigerman

Archeworks Headquarters, Chicago.

Founded by architect Stanley Tigerman and interior designer Eva Madox, Archeworks is an Alternative Design School that aims to provide a curriculum which responsibly addresses contemporary needs in society and the urban environment. This new head-quarters by Tigerman is a 5,325 sq.ft space under a bridge.

TOP: Plan. ABOVE: EXterior, showing the shed structure below a main freeway into Chicago. Photograph, Hedrich Blessing.

Harry Seidler

Horizon Apartments, Sydney.

Clorindo Testa

Sketch.

Alain Sarfati

Théâtre de la Cité, Toulouse.

The walkway leading to the small hall.
Photograph, Philippe Ruault.

Solsona

Piletas de Mar del Plata.

Rob Krier

"It is striking that all the urban visions of the past hundred years were based on abstract intellectual theories about the functioning of the urban fabric. These diverse concepts of urban design share one thing in common: their intentional departure from the traditional European city – the kind of city increasingly seen as a very desirable place to live and work. None of these familiar cities and towns originated in our century. They are not the brain-children or the products of an abstract idea. Rather, they derive from a basic universal principle, namely perimeter block development that results from the placement of like individual units in a row, on parcels of property with quiet inner courtyards, fronted by commercial streets."

Rudy Ricciotti

Collège d'Auriol.

Rob Krier

Kirchsteigfeld, Potsdam, Germany, a new town of 10,000 inhabitants.

Francis Soler

Apartment building, rue Emile Durkheim, Paris.

Consumer Society:
Myths and Structures
by **Jean Baudrillard**

Symbolic Exchange and Death
by **Jean Baudrillard**

Jean Baudrillard, Art and Artefact
by **Jean Baudrillard**
Sage Publications

The *Consumer Society: Myths and Structures*, Baudrillard's most organised examination of mass media culture, and the meaning of leisure and anomie in affluent societies is finally available in English, by Sage Publications. And it still reads very well over a quarter of a century after its initial publication. (*La societé de consommation*, Editions Denöel, 1970).

The book that made a radical break with the productivist orientation that predominated at the time of its original publication, is still very influential, especially in the United States. Its value today, lies both on the fact that it is relatively timeless – it will probably be relevant for as long as consumerism is a dominant aspect of the social world – and on that it shows a theorist (and a theory) in transition. Furthermore, it is a work that can be read profitably for theoretical perspectives that can help us to think better about the consumer society.

The translation includes a preface by George Ritzer that attempts to put Baudrillard's ideas into a contemporary perspective. In his analysis he remarks that: "while from one angle there is theoretical richness to be found, from another a range of theoretical perspectives can be seen as coexisting uncomfortably." But even if some of these early Baudrillard positions seem sometimes problematic they help us approach his current work. As George Ritzer concludes: "In

exploring the weaknesses we must not lose sight of the fact that the Consumer Society is a significant contribution to social theory, and Jean Baudrillard demonstrates here something that was to become even clearer as his work progressed in the ensuing decade or so – that he is a major social theorist."

It is not the first time that Sage Publications offer a first English translation of Baudrillard's work: In 1993 they published *Symbolic Exchange and Death*, (*L' échange symbolic et la mort*, Editions Gallimard, 1976), where Baudrillard provides a source for the redefinition of contemporary social thought. It leads the reader on an tour that encompasses the end of marxism, the enchantment of fashion, the body and sex, economic versus symbolic exchange and their differing effects on rituals of death.

But most significantly, *Symbolic Exchange and Death* represents Baudrillard's fullest elaboration on the concept of the three concepts of simulacra, defining the historical passage from production to reproduction to simulation.

As a companion to these translations comes *Jean Baudrillard, Art and Artefact*, edited by Nicholas Zurbrugg. This collection of essays, writings and interviews attempts to offer a reappraisal of Baudrillard's thoughts on the image, radical illusion and media culture. Nicholas Zurbrugg thinks that the book contains "readings-in-progress of Baudrillard, and readings against Baudrillard, but in either case, attempts to respond 'on the scale' of the Baudrillardian wager, openly and audaciously, rather than conservatively and defensively".

In this book Baudrillard's catalytic provocations on the issues of urban reality, aesthetics, virtual reality and new media technologies, are put

for the first time under the perspective of what he calls the "stunning clarity" of the photographic image, in the light of his practice as a photographer.

Baudrillard's Challenge, A Feminist Reading
By **Victoria Grace**
Routledge, London

Baudrillard has a broad influence on many fields of theoretical studies. But his significance has been largely ignored by feminist theorists. In *Baudrillard's Challenge* Victoria Grace deploys her understanding of Baudrillard's work to further the development of feminist theory.

Digital Creativity:
Architecture, Landscape, Design
Proceedings of Greenwich 2000:
Digital Creativity Symposium
The University of Greenwich

Covering the themes "Algorithmic Design: Problem Solving, Form and Space", "Computers and the Urban Environment", "The Impact of Digital Technology on the Professions of the Built Environment", "Computer Visualisation and Animation", "Digital Aspects of Landscape Environments", "Creativity in Teaching and Learning Practice" and "Creative Process and Design" this volume is a multi-faceted presentation of the current international research on the relation between design process and digital technology.

Principles of Modern Architecture
By **Christian Norberg-Schulz**
Andreas Papadakis Publisher

In this concise account of what the Modern Movement really wanted and what it achieved Christian

Norberg-Schulz investigates the basic principles of modern architecture including the "free plan" and the "open form," as well as the manifestations of modern life in the terms "house", "institution" and "city". He also discusses the problems of "regionalism" and "monumentality" and concludes with a summing up of the endeavours of modern architecture under the heading "The New Place".

Seven Experimental Architectural Essays on and by Hiromi Fujii, The Recent Architecture of Hiromi Fujii

Organised as a catalogue of an architectural exhibition on Hiromi Fujii which was held as one of the events that celebrated the 250th Anniversary of the Moscow Institute of Architecture. (See Cosmorama, pages 102-104)

London Suburbs
Introduction by **Andrew Saint**
Merrell Holberton Publishers Ltd, London

Regarded by some as idyllic, by others as tormenting, the suburban ideal has impulses steeped in architectural, social and historical significance. The suburb also has a fabric, a real form and an architectural character. *London Suburbs* examines this heritage of the dynamic story of London's suburban expansion, a complex result of chance, planning, geography, transport innovations and architects' ideas. In chronologically arranged chapters, fully illustrated with maps, plans painting and photographs, the book depicts the many stages of London's outward growth, the imposition or the trickle-down of social and architectural ideas, its history of individual and public initiatives, its inner and outer rings, villages, centres and districts.

Stylistic Cold Wars:
Betjeman versus Pevsner
By **Timothy Mowl**
John Murray Publishers Ltd, London

John Betjeman and Nikolaus Pevsner were opposites. Both, however, had a profound influence on the way Britain looks today. In *Stylistic Cold Wars*, Timothy Mowl charts their spontaneous rise as style warriors. In Pevsner's case, his transformation form a respected German art historian to the determined exponent of international modernism, intent on the imposition of a functional townscape upon post-war Britain. In Betjeman's, his conversion from idealistic young journalist, acclaiming the dawn of the machine age, concrete, steel and all, to the great lyric poet who effectively launched the "Heritage Industry".

Richard Rogers:
Complete Works, Volume One
By **Kenneth Powell**
Phaidon

In this first volume, *Richard Rogers: Complete Works* features all of Rogers' early work, including projects from Yale with Norman Foster and Team 4, his partnerships with Sue Rogers and Renzo Piano, through to the philosophy of Richard Rogers Partnership. Kenneth Powell discusses the projects and builds up a portrait of the work and the people involved during the period, from 1961 to 1987.

Tate Modern, The Handbook
Edited by **Iwona Blazwick** and **Simon Wilson**
Tate Publishing

The Handbook is a complement to a visit to Tate Modern. Like the gallery, it presents 20th century art

through four classic themes, the Nude, Landscape, Still life and History painting, tracing their continuation and transformation through the century and discussing their re-emergence in modern art as the Body, the Environment, Real life and Society. The concluding section is an A to Z of one hundred of the foremost artists in one of the world's leading collections of 20th-century art. In this way, the Handbook is not just about the Tate Modern collection, but it is also a flexible tool for the understanding of modern art.

David Hockney, Espace / Paysage
Éditions du Centre Pompidou

This catalogue of the exhibition *David Hockney, Espace / Paysage* follows Hockney's work from the early sixties to the late nineties, moving from his early paintings to the in-depth analysis of perspective in his latest work. With extensive entries on the fifty or so paintings exhibited at the Pompidou, and with analytical texts on Hockney's "inverse perspective" this volume is a concise and complete account of the painter's research.

Art Nouveau 1890-1914
Edited by **Paul Greenhalgh**
V&A Publications

Coinciding with the V&A exhibition, this book deals with Art Nouveau as an international phenomenon and explores how the artists and designers who created Art Nouveau aimed to transform the world, by challenging convention and embracing modernity, as well as the impact of the movement right across Europe and America. The careers of leading figures are analysed and the style's dramatic demise is examined.

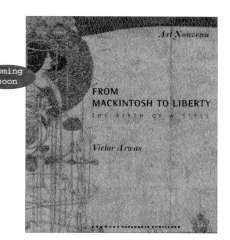

coming soon

A R T

Art Nouveau:
From Mackintosh to Liberty:
The Birth of a Style
by **Victor Arwas**

ISBN: 1 901092 19 4
305 x 262 mm, 200 pages
including 96 pages in colour
Publication: September 2000
Paperback with flaps: £27.50

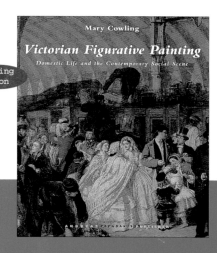

coming soon

new

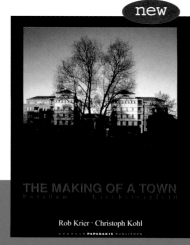

new

Victorian Figurative Painting,
Domestic Life and the Contemporary
Social Scene
by **Mary Cowling**

ISBN: 1 901092 29 1
300 x 252 mm, 200 pages, 200
illustrations including 80 in colour
Publication: August 2000
Paperback with flaps: £27.50

Principles of Modern Architecture
by **Christian Norberg-Schulz**

ISBN: 1 901092 24 0
300 x 240 mm, 136 pages,
over 200 illustrations
Paperback with flaps: £19.50
available now

The Making of a Town
by **Rob Krier** and **Christoph Kohl**

ISBN: 1 901092 15 1
300 x 240 mm, 224 pages,
290 illustrations, mostly in colour
Hardback: £35.00
available now

THEORY & DESIGN

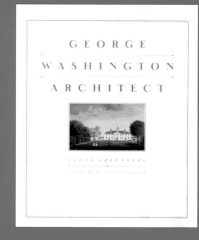

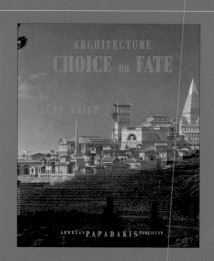

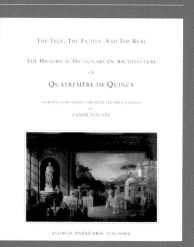

NA**MONOGRAPHS**

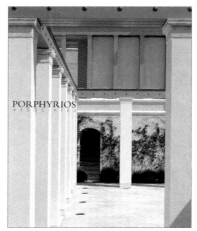

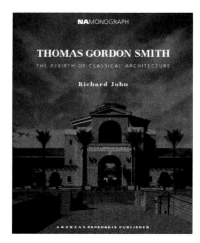

NEW**ARCHITECTURE**

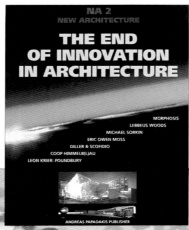

COMING
SOON ▶

NA6
The City: Future Uncertain

ISBN: 1 901092 31 3
300 x 240 mm, 144 pages
over 150 illustrations
Publication: September
Paperback with flaps:
£17.50
A presentation of the most
important of the 35 country
exhibits including the work
of more than 200 inter-
national architects
exhibiting at this year's
Venice Architecture
Biennale on the theme
"Cities: less aesthetics,
more ethics."

LESS AESTHETICS MORE ETHICS

la Biennale di Venezia

I would like to order the following books:

DECORATIVE ARTS

____	Victor Arwas	THE ART OF GLASS	hb 1 901092 00 3	$35.00 / £17.50
____	Victor Arwas	ART NOUVEAU FROM MACKINTOSH		
		TO LIBERTY: THE BIRTH OF A STYLE	pb 1 901092 19 4	$35.00 / £17.50*
____	Mary Cowling	VICTORIAN FIGURATIVE PAINTING I	pb 1 901092 29 1	$35.00 / £17.50*

ARCHITECTURE

____	Allan Greenberg	GEORGE WASHINGTON, ARCH	hb 1 901092 18 6	$55.00 / £35.00
____	Vilma Hastaoglou	RESTRUCTURING THE CITY	pb 1 901092 16 X	$48.00 / £30.00
____	Léon Krier	ARCHITECTURE: CHOICE OR FATE	pb 1 901092 03 8	$39.00 / £24.95
____	Rob Krier & C. Kohl	THE MAKING OF A TOWN	hb 1 901092 15 1	$55.00 / £35.00
____	Sebastian Loew	PROMOTION OF ARCHITECTURE	pb 1 901092 02 X	$12.00 / £ 7.95
____	C. Norberg-Schulz	PRINCIPLES OF MODERN ARCH.	pb 1 901092 24 0	$35.00 / £19.50
____	Demetri Porphyrios	CLASSICAL ARCHITECTURE	pb 1 901092 06 2	$35.00 / £19.50
____	Elisabeth Tostrup	ARCHITECTURE AND RHETORIC	hb 1 901092 05 4	$55.00 / £35.00
____	Samir Younés	QUATREMERE DE QUINCY	hb 1 901092 17 8	$55.00 / £35.00*

NEW ARCHITECTURE

____	NA 1	REACHING FOR THE FUTURE	pb 1 901092 01 1	$27.50 / £17.50
____	NA 2	THE END OF INNOVATION	pb 1 901092 09 7	$27.50 / £17.50
____	NA 3	JAPAN AT THE CUTTING EDGE	pb 1 901092 10 0	$27.50 / £17.50
____	NA 4	UK2K	pb 1 901092 28 3	$27.50 / £17.50
____	NA 5	TRUTH, RADICALITY AND BEYOND	pb 1 901092 12 7	$27.50 / £17.50*
____	NA 6	THE CITY: FUTURE UNCERTAIN	pb 1 901092 31 3	$27.50 / £17.50*
____	NA 7	THE VIRTUAL IS REAL	pb 1 901092 26 7	$27.50 / £17.50*

NA MONOGRAPHS

____	NAM1	PETER PRAN	pb 1 901092 07 0	$37.50 / £22.50
			hb 1 901092 08 9	$45.00 / £27.50
____	NAM2	PORPHYRIOS ASSOCIATES	pb 1 901092 13 5	$45.00 / £27.50
			hb 1 901092 14 3	$55.00 / £35.00
____	NAM3	THOMAS GORDON SMITH AND	pb 1 901092 21 6	$45.00 / £27.50*
		THE REBIRTH OF CLASSICAL ARCH	hb 1 901092 22 4	$55.00 / £35.00*

NA SUBSCRIPTIONS

____	Full Rate	6 numbers (inc. postage)	$130.00 / £90.00
____	Student Rate	6 numbers (inc. postage)	$ 90.00 / £60.00

* Newest titles   Please add £3.00 postage per volume for the UK; £3.50 for Europe; £7.50 for the USA and Far East

Payment is enclosed by Cheque / Money Order / Draft $......................................

£......................................

Please charge £ ....   to my credit card

Account No...   Expiry date ....

Name ....

Address ....

....

....

Signature ....

A N D R E A S   P A P A D A K I S   P U B L I S H E R
107 Park Street, London W1Y 3FB
Tel. +44 (0)20 7499 0444   Fax +44 (0)20 7499 0222

subscription and order form

Cumulative index

The prefix indicates the number of the issue:
1 - NA1 REACHING FOR THE FUTURE
2 - NA2 THE END OF INNOVATION
3 - NA3 JAPAN AT THE CUTTING EDGE
4 - NA4 UK2K
5 - NA5 TRUTH, RADICALITY AND BEYOND
Extensive presentation is indicated in bold.